THE FIRST COMPUTER BOOK:

A SIMPLE GUIDE FOR ADULTS

GENE BROWN

BANTAM BOOKS
TORONTO · NEW YORK · LONDON · SYDNEY

Book Design by David M. Nehila

Technical illustrations by Alphonse Tvaryanas
Chapter illustrations by Marty Norman

THE FRIENDLY COMPUTER BOOK: A SIMPLE GUIDE FOR ADULTS

A Bantam Book/September 1983

All rights reserved.
Copyright © 1983 by Cloverdale Press.

Produced by Cloverdale Press
133 Fifth Avenue
New York, New York 10003

ISBN 0-553-23872-8

Published simultaneously in the United States and Canada

PRINTED IN THE UNITED STATES OF AMERICA

O   0 9 8 7 6 5 4 3 2

ACKNOWLEDGMENTS

I am grateful to Susan Osborn, a fine writer and editor and a good friend, who encouraged me to undertake this project and bolstered my spirits whenever the going got rough.

I would like to thank Jeffrey and Daniel Weiss of Cloverdale Press for giving me the opportunity to write this book. Ted Stevenson's critical perspective improved the organization of the manuscript at several points, and Nathan Hull's knowledge of computers saved me from many factual errors.

Barbara Becker, my editor, did service above and beyond the call of duty. Her professional skills and enthusiasm were a constant source of assistance and encouragement in the final shaping of the manuscript.

Marilyn Annan and her colleagues at the *New York Times* Reference Library—Paul Greenfeder, Bill Anderson, Ann Harvey, and Gray Peart—were friends and helpers in this, as in previous endeavors.

For information and/or research material, I owe thanks to: Frank Abenante, Joseph Arcaro, Michael Bader, Alan Greengrass, Edwin Hellgoth, Bob Rumerman, Larry and Sylviane Simonberg, Joanne Soderman, and Lieselotte Winters.

Eve Marie Rommel read much of the manuscript, made many useful suggestions, and through her patience and support contributed more to its completion than she will ever realize.

To My Parents

CONTENTS

INTRODUCTION

Children are increasingly at home in the world of computers, which can seem so alien to their elders. Many schools now introduce their students to computers in kindergarten. They grow up wise in the ways of this new technology and sense nothing inherently contradictory in the term "personal computer." They write programs almost as naturally as their parents wrote compositions about what happened during summer vacation. "They know what computers can and cannot do," says IBM's Louis Robinson, "while adults still regard them [computers] as omnipotent."

"It's dumb. I have to tell it everything," says a ten-year-old who already knows computers. Why are those of us not socialized to the world of bits and bytes so quick to give the computer more than its due? Part of the explanation must certainly lie in our misconceptions about what a computer is and does— that the machine "thinks," or spends most of its time manipulating fierce-looking equations, or is part of a system which is essentially infallible (or else consciously and malevolently fallible). In the back of some of our minds may even be the thought that the computer is somehow better than we, able to transcend our limitations while having none of its own. Unfortunately, the jargon-filled pronouncements of many experts in the field have served only to reinforce these notions.

While some of the things that worry us about computers are actually a product of our imaginations, other problems are quite real.

For example, their effect on how we make our

living—and in some cases on our ability to continue to make a living—is only too evident. The now-ubiquitous computer terminal has changed both the office and the factory. Typists are becoming "word processors," and filing clerks find themselves working in data processing departments carting around reams of accordion-like paper with holes in the edges. Many unlucky production-line workers discover to their horror that automation has made them expendable.

In the title role of the film *The Graduate*, Dustin Hoffman was advised that plastics was the field to be in; today it would be computers. Classified ads are now filled with offers for programmers and systems analysts, the former starting at over fifteen thousand dollars a year and the latter getting even bigger money after only a few years of experience. At a time when switching careers has become fashionable, computer technology is the career that many are switching to. And yet the vast majority of us are unlikely to have the opportunity to learn very much about computers. Thus the technology that dominates our lives is likely to remain mystifying.

And in our society's pell-mell rush to computerize, it's easy to feel somewhat bulldozed as the mass media bombards us with images of technological revolution. Recently, for example, *Newsweek* solemnly intoned that "Computer experts see only one major impediment to the rapid growth of the information age: resistance to the technology by an adult generation that fears it"—implying that we had better get wise or get out of the way.

In these still-early days of the computer era, it seems that more frequently it is the young who have the opportunity to obtain the hands-on experience required for real computer familiarity; adults must "get it secondhand," or read about it. These days, experience comes with youth.

This book will demystify the computer. It will tell you what it is (and isn't), where it came from, how it works, and how it's being used in all facets of your life. It is written for you, in a style that is no more complicated than that of your daily newspaper. The only assumption it makes is that you are curious about this preeminent tool of our age.

CHAPTER 1

COMPUTERS:
THE MYTH
AND THE REALITY

"Automation Claims Another Job" was the *New York Times* headline on October 4, 1963. The employee's working career had lasted all of twelve years, although this relatively brief time on the job had yielded greatly increased productivity for the employer. Dedication and loyalty had never been in question: how many workers put in twenty-four hours a day, every day? Luther Hodges, then secretary of commerce, presided at the retirement ceremony at the Bureau of the Census. As he groped for the right words of appreciation, someone at the back of the room said, "How about giving it a gold watch?" "It" was UNIVAC I, the most famous computer of its time.

UNIVAC did not go quietly into the night. It was granted a few last words, and it rose to the occasion: "The program just completed, a sample revision of construction statistics, is the final run on UNIVAC I, serial number one. This computer has been in service for 12 years and 6 months and has produced over 73,500 hours of operation use. On this date, October 3, 1963, the Bureau of the Census transfers custody of this machine to the Smithsonian Institution. The end."

The first electronic digital computers—the kind of machine we would recognize today as the modern computer—were built during and shortly after World War II to provide the vast calculating power and speed needed to crack secret enemy codes, plot the trajectory of artillery shells, and design the first atomic weapons. UNIVAC, on the other hand, was the first computer made for universal use.

Introduced in 1951, UNIVAC really came into the public eye the following year when it was used on television to help tabulate presidential election returns. Although this computer was originally purchased by the federal government, within a few years the machine came into more general use. In 1954, General Electric became the first private company to own one. UNIVAC was put to work preparing the payroll at GE's Kentucky office, and with that the era of business data processing was born—but only "after a certain amount of agony and mishap," as one observer noted.

We've come a long way since UNIVAC. The 1949 prediction of *Popular Mechanics* that eventually computers would "only have one thousand vacuum tubes and perhaps weigh only one and one-half tons" might seem pretty strange to the schoolchildren next door whose Apple, Atari, or VIC-20 sits on a table next to the television. Their parents may recall a time when a computer was as big as a one-bedroom apartment; today's students know the machine as just another electronic device that, increasingly, is likely to be found around the house.

Miracle or Menace?

Today computers are the mainstay of much of our civilization. It is hard to imagine large corporations—and small businesses too, for that matter—keeping track of inventory, making out payrolls, tracking accounts receivable and payable, analyzing current sales figures, and projecting future ones without the use of computers. The computerized mailing lists that permit automatic sales targeting of special interest groups are the basis of the lucrative direct mail trade. Business records stored as computerized data on disks and tape would strangle the modern company with tons of paper and a heavy burden of labor costs, were they to be handled as they were before the arrival of the computer.

Computers have become an important part of all the sciences, from those that look toward the outer edges of the universe to the most earth-bound. Computers navigate our spacecraft and monitor and control the complex systems that make astronautics a science rather than science fiction. Geological formations on this planet are analyzed by computer for the possible presence of oil deposits. Maps that once were drawn laboriously by hand are now prepared by these machines.

We live better and longer because of computers. Many medical lab tests can be performed faster, in greater volume, and just as accurately by computer as by hand. Computer-controlled patient-monitoring devices in hospitals free nurses for other tasks. Diagnostic devices such as the CAT (computerized axial tomography) scan have made much exploratory surgery unnecessary.

In our daily lives we make use of countless devices based on computers. When we are out our calls may be handled by a telephone answering system. We ride in safe, computer-controlled elevators, type on electronic typewriters, and choose a TV station by pushing a button connected to a small computer in the set. When we go out to the movies we may see a film with special effects created through the use of a computer, and in the lobby we play video games on a computer.

We do things more quickly, more efficiently, less expensively, and on a larger scale because of the computer. In fact, much of what is done with the computer could be accomplished in no other way. One could easily conclude, then, that this machine is one of the blessings of twentieth-century technology. But while some people might think so, many others would disagree.

While the computer has solved many problems, it has also created quite a few of its own. It is often used to store vast quantities of information that can be summoned up in a few seconds. Although that's convenient, it is also potentially dangerous. Personal records kept by government and business have been expanding as our ability to store and gain quick access to them has increased. But how much information on ourselves do we want made available on a moment's notice—and to whom?

Bureaucracies that tended to treat people as numbers even before computers were widely available have since found it even easier to regard them simply as bits of data. We have set up big, complicated systems of record keeping, but when the system goes awry there often seems to be no satisfactory—and acceptable—way of getting a grievance redressed. "Do not bend, fold, spindle, or mutilate," we have been warned when handling IBM cards—when in fact we might have been thinking of breaking, kicking, throttling, or smashing.

While an increasingly automated society may make life easier, it also makes us more vulnerable. What happens if we become totally dependent on these machines and they break down? What happens to the people displaced by automation? Our nuclear attack warning system depends on computers: what if a false signal is given? In fact, it's happened more than once.

Our unease with the role computers play in our lives is often expressed in ways other than concern over the machine's social, economic, and political effects. On the one hand, computers are often seen as omnipotent devices whose words and numbers are not to be questioned, machines that are too good at what they do. On the other hand, computers are frequently cast as clumsy and error-prone. Or as the sign on a desk at one of this country's most prominent newspapers states: "To err is human, to really foul things up requires a computer."

Computers are used to check up on us; they make sure that we stay on the straight and narrow. They monitor many aspects of our daily lives and they judge us in terms of numbers. Who can argue with a number? Internal Revenue Service computers, for example, automatically check the numbers on a tax return to see if they exceed the average figures for a person with that income and those deductions. If a return deviates from the norm it is pulled out and given special attention. It's like being graded on a curve at school, but this time a high mark could mean big trouble.

Employees of a large company are often blessed with a WATS (Wide Area Telephone Service) system. Some may think that long-distance telephone calls are free for the making and that the company could care less about regular calls to friends and relatives across the country. Not so. Although the company pays a flat rate for long-distance phone service, that rate can go up if the average number of such calls per month increases over a certain period of time. Some firms are using computers to thwart the use of this self-appropriated fringe benefit, and a too-frequent caller is bound to get caught. A log is kept of all long-distance calls. The computer then rearranges the information; one way is to group together all the calls to any one number and check them to see from whose extensions they were placed.

Our number may also come up on the road. Computers not only process traffic tickets—they also help to create them. Unlucky motorists who were caught speeding in the last few years may already have met VASCAR (Visual Average Speed Computer and Recorder). VASCAR quickly calculates a car's speed based on how long it took the car to travel between two predetermined, monitored points. It is accurate to one-tenth of a mile per hour.

Garbage In/Garbage Out: What You Give Is What You Get

Recently a major American bank spotted an error in a complicated program (the instructions that tell a computer what to do) before much damage could be done. Bank customers then received form letters explaining that there could be errors in their statements. The letters declared, ''Since they're programmed by people, computers are only human. . . ."

Most computer "malfunctioning" really involves misuse of a computer by a human, but the habit of attributing errors to the computer rather than the person using it has already become deeply embedded in our society. Did anyone ever blame a poorly typed letter on a "typewriter error"? "Computer Error . . .," began a recent *New York Times* headline about a foul-up that cost the U.S. government thirty-five million dollars. "Computer error," echoed the first sentence of the story. "An incorrect computer entry," began the second paragraph, as the truth started to surface: still another misuse of the machine rather than a "glitch" in the computer itself.

The source of a computer-generated error could be either the machine itself or the person programming or operating it. Someone inconvenienced by such an error often finds it easier to assume the machine was at fault. The computer goofed: what can you do?

We all know a few horror stories about how a computer made life difficult for us or somebody we know. Credit card companies seem especially vulnerable to these computer "glitches." One person who kept receiving bills for $00.00, month after month, finally stopped the nonsense by sending the company a check for that amount—only to receive another bill, this one for a late payment fee.

Bureaucratic "procedures" can clog up even the most reliable of computers. A famous gourmet magazine once wrote itself a recipe for disaster when it dispatched a form letter to the sender of a gift subscription advising that if problems arose, any correspondence should include the file number of the subscription. The number was: 0 580004 BGL—03135092 LI49E31113 T8 2Y 0008953—a number far longer than anything needed to identify one subscriber. The machine was only too happy to cook up this hash. But if blame were to be placed it should have been on the system designer, not the computer.

Some time ago, astronauts L. Gordon Cooper and Charles Conrad splashed down 103 miles of ocean away from their target. The computer that calculated their landing place had performed its job perfectly. But the instructions that fired their rockets in orbit, slowed them down, and helped start their descent assumed that the earth made one complete turn on its axis every twenty-four hours. If this were in fact the case, we wouldn't need a leap year every fourth year.

"GIGO," the professionals call it: "garbage in/garbage out." Computer accuracy is dependent on the accuracy of the information humans feed it, so misinformation given to the machine will produce inaccurate results. A computer is just like any other tool: if it's misused, it can't get the job done.

Sometimes, of course, things seem hopelessly out of hand. Perhaps no other organization, public or private, has been noted for as much computer-generated grief as the Social Security Administration. To serve over 150 million people with a computer system that is more than twenty-five years old (although it's being gradually replaced) is risky business indeed. One man truly endured the trials of a saint when he sought for five years to prove to the agency that, the decisions of its computers notwithstanding, he was not dead. Finally his plight came to the attention of John Svahn, then head of the agency. "I personally tried to get that case fixed," Svahn admitted, "and I failed."

Can These Things Think?

Computers are marvelous machines that can deal with all kinds of data—in fact they are the only kind of machine that runs on information. This has led to many misconceptions about what computers really are and what they are capable of doing. The strangeness of computers—compared to other machines with which we are more familiar—has given them an air of mystery and has made it easy for us to believe almost anything we read—or imagine, for that matter—about them.

Even the hard-headed among us are likely to go soft in their resolve when faced with a powerful machine they don't understand. According to a study made by the management consultants from Booz, Allen and Hamilton, about one-third of all business executives truly fear the computer. These people apparently anticipate a loss of control; they imagine that they will become so drawn into the workings of the machine that they will be taken over. Where once *they* made the decisions, now they see themselves as mere "information conduits." (They also find the keyboard used for entering data and instructions forbidding: it suggests a status much lower in the business world than they have attained—and besides, many of them can't type.)

For the average person, there is another thing about computers that often seems especially upsetting. Computers are capable of making logical decisions by comparing one number to another and then doing one thing if the first number is larger than the second, doing something else if the numbers are equal, and taking yet a third course if the second number is larger than the first. That's a pretty powerful thing for a machine to be doing.

Researchers in the field of "artificial intelligence" have been exploring the limits of the computer's ability to make even more complex decisions based on such comparisons. Some have suggested that there are virtually no limits to what computers can do in this area. The claims of these experts and even the very name of the field suggest something that frightens many people: that the machine thinks.

The Myth
And the Reality

Young people today are learning about and working with computers, starting in grade school. They know the computer as an interesting, flexible, and useful tool. But their elders probably formed their ideas about computers based on movies in which the computer was portrayed as a huge box set in an antiseptically white room. Surrounded by banks of flashing red lights, it was connected to large tape units that spun with a soft whir, stopped with a clack, and then reversed direction to spin, stop, and start again. Typically, white-coated scientists hovered about the machine, silent, clipboards in hand, faces betraying concern. At best the computer was awesome; more often than not it proved to be malevolent, out of control, or consciously intent on taking over.

For those of us past our mid-twenties the computer is probably a machine that has always been somewhat physically removed from us. We've flown in a plane, driven a car, gone to the movies, and watched TV. But we haven't done anything with computers; if anything, they seem to be doing things to us. Only recently have computers, in their "personal" version, begun to be common material objects in our lives.

Computers—mysterious, powerful, willful, all-but-incomprehensible, and more than a little frightening. They are everywhere and we interact with them in some way every day. Still, they are electronic strangers in our lives. Where did they come from? How do they work? What can they do—and not do?

In reality the computer is no more mysterious than that other prime example of twentieth-century technology, the automobile. Cars have shrunk our world; they have enabled us to enjoy suburban living and in general have made life easier. But because we have sometimes let automobile technology dominate our lives—rather than the reverse—our use of the auto has also ravaged the landscape and caused tens of thousands of traffic fatalities every year.

Like the automobile, the computer is just a neutral piece of machinery. We can understand it and use it intelligently; or we can fear it and use it blindly and ineffectively. Knowledge of these machines should not be just for the young. It's time we all knew something about the computer in our lives.

CHAPTER 2

I∎∎⁰⁰ ⁰⁰⁰I ⁰⁰⁰⁰ ⁰I∎∎⁰⁰ ⁰∎∎I

FROM COUNTING
ON DIGITS
TO DIGITAL
COUNTING

An inventor tinkers in his garage with a few pipes, some wire, and an old engine. One night he accidentally crosses two wires and—Eureka!—he produces a new machine for mankind.

In fact, technology does not usually advance this way. More often, modifications are made to things we already know and use, and those changes are usually called forth by practical necessity. In the case of the computer, better ways of calculating have been developed in response to needs ranging from those of ancient traders to today's planetary scientists exploring outer space.

Although the computer evolved over quite a long period of time, its story really focuses on a few key improvements in the way that man has dealt with numbers. Unlike the functioning of a computer, which is orderly, exact, and predictable, the development of this machine—as is true for much technology—was haphazard, circumstantial, and highlighted by a few individuals who were not without their own eccentricities.

Early Counting Methods

Our reliance on numbers is an outgrowth of our continuing effort to control and put into perspective the various elements in our lives. The objects around us are not naturally set out in groups with labels indicating how many there are: *we* impose numbers on the outside world. And although even in ancient times numbers were sacred in and of themselves and could bring good luck or ill fortune, most often they were simply used for counting.

Almost certainly, the first counting was done on man's fingers; hence the dual meaning of the word "digit." Early in its history, each world culture seems to have developed its own symbolic way of expressing numbers, some of these systems easier to work with than others. The Yancos, for example, a tribe found in the Amazon Basin, symbolized their numbers in words. Their word for three is "poettarrarorincoaroac"—and that's as high as they count. (Even Roman numerals, with which we are all familiar, look very impressive carved in granite but are nearly impossible to multiply or divide.)

Commerce was carried on in the ancient world with the aid of a somewhat convenient method of counting things: physical objects representing the items being counted were used on devices like counting boards, which employed chips; the more familiar abacus used beads. Each of these crude calculators counted by tens, in a logical imitation of the natural finger-counting system.

But there was something even more interesting about these primitive computers. If you were going to count only by tens, how were you going to record large numbers? The solution was simple but elegant. It involved the idea of "place" and the use of the zero as an important number.

Strangely enough, people continued to use their fingers for expressing and manipulating even large numbers until just a few centuries ago. This kind of calculation involved the use of many symbols made

In some parts of the world—primarily the Orient—the abacus is still the basic computing device. Each row represents a "place," starting on the right with units. Each bead above the bar stands for five; the beads below each represent one. Beads are moved towards the bar to record a number.

with the fingers—not just holding up a few fingers to express a quantity. It was, in fact, something akin to sign language, but it was not terribly practical, since series of calculations—particularly if done quickly—could require near contortions.

During the medieval period, the introduction into Western Europe of so-called Arabic numerals (which actually originated in India) was a big step toward making calculations easier. A ninth-century book on arithmetic, written by a Persian known in Latin as Algorismus (a corruption of al-Khuwarizmi), appears to have been the West's initial introduction to the numbers we are familiar with. And there things stood for several hundred years because there was no incentive to increase computational powers. Educated men and women knew nothing more about mathematics than elementary counting and perhaps a little addition and subtraction. By our standards, they were mathematically illiterate.

Napier's Powers

The exploration and navigation of the world and the beginning of modern scientific observation that came with the Renaissance brought with them a need to make more exact and quicker calculations than even the wisest men had heretofore been capable of doing. John Napier, an Englishman who lived in the second half of the sixteenth century and who spent much of his time calculating, found to his chagrin that he was "subject to many slippery errors." Computing correctly was important enough to him that he made it his business to get a more solid grip on the world of numbers.

One of the brightest men of his time, Napier was clever as well as intelligent. He came up with the idea of dealing with large numbers by representing them as powers of smaller numbers. If, for example, he wanted to represent the number 144 in a long calculation, he asked himself how many times a given number might have to be multiplied by itself to get 144. If he were using 12 as the base of his system, the answer would be one time. He could do this for each number in his calculations, thus ending up with smaller, easier-to-handle numbers corresponding to all the larger numbers he had begun with. Napier devised a set of rules for adding, subtracting, multiplying, and dividing these numbers so that the results were the

Napier's Bones, the forerunner of the modern slide rule.

same as if he had worked with the original figures.

Then he came up with a method of inscribing these smaller numbers on sticks and using the sticks together to perform calculations by sliding them back and forth, matching the numbers and moving them apart to arrive at an answer. "Napier's Bones," as the device was called, was improved after his death by Henry Briggs, another Englishman, who systematized the numbers to make them all powers of 10. By 1628, the powers of 10 corresponding to every number from 1 to 100,000 had been calculated. The system became known as logarithms and the table of values was called a logarithmic (log) table. Napier's Bones was further refined until it eventually became the modern slide rule.

The main problem with logs is that they are not

always neat. The log of 100 is 2, because $10^2 = 10 \times 10 = 100$—which is somewhat neat. But what's the log of 79, for example? It's going to be a 1 with a long decimal after it. A slide rule can handle this, although not with absolute precision, since a slide rule is an analog computer that makes a comparison by representing a quantity (in this case, the log of 79) in terms of another physical quantity (the distance between two scratches on a piece of wood). Theoretically, a mechanical calculator should be more accurate, and certainly quicker and easier to use.

By the seventeenth century the absence of such a calculator was keenly felt as interest in astronomy and the other sciences increased. At that time it took astronomer Johannes Kepler four years to calculate the orbit of Mars (a task which a properly programmed modern computer could accomplish in a few seconds). Any device that could increase the speed and accuracy of such calculations would certainly have been well received.

Pascal and Leibniz

The first accurate and completely reliable machine of this type was invented in 1642 by the French mathematician and philosopher Blaise Pascal. Pascal did not attend school; he was educated at home by his lawyer-mathematician father. The calculator he built, the Pascaline, was made of a series of ten-toothed wheels, each representing a column or place—1s, 10s, 100s, etc. After a wheel in any column had been

Each of the wheels on the Pascaline was linked to the one next to it. Turning a wheel past the ninth digit caused its neighbor to turn and register one more, thus carrying the number to the next place.

turned to the ninth digit, the next turn of that wheel would rotate the wheel in the next column one place, thus carrying one digit over, just like the odometer in your automobile. Thomas Hobbes, the political philosopher, in a remarkable observation that prefigured the world of computers to come, said of the Pascaline that "Brass and iron have been invested with the function of brain. . . ."

Gottfried Leibniz, a great mathematician and philosopher, thought it "unworthy of excellent men to lose hours like slaves in the labor of calculation which could safely be relegated to anyone else if machines were used." The thought impelled him to design a calculator that could multiply and divide as well as perform the addition and subtraction accomplished by the Pascaline. But contemporary machine technology was not precise enough to embody his ideas.

The Analytical Machine

Charles Babbage's study of early mail-delivery systems in his native England resulted in the formation of the first modern postal service. The speedometer was another product of his fertile imagination, and he invented the cowcatcher on the front of old locomotives. But these pale in the face of his greatest accomplishment, for if anyone can be called the inventor of the computer, it is he.

Charles Babbage, "inventor" of the modern computer.

Photo courtesy of IBM Corporation

Babbage was born in 1792, the son of a banker. At an early age he displayed an intense and persistent curiosity. He insisted that the workings of his toys be explained to him; if he was not satisfied that he understood the true nature of their innards, he ripped them open to see for himself.

Shortly after he graduated from Cambridge, Babbage was recognized as one of the great mathematical geniuses of his age, and he was appointed to the Chair of Mathematics at Cambridge that had been held by Isaac Newton. Like Leibniz, Babbage found calculating an "intolerable labor and fatiguing monotony." He was a stickler for accuracy; imprecision with numbers drove him into a dither.

He lived in an age when Britain's sea power was at its height; anything that could make navigational calculations easier would have been as useful to his society as new and cheaper fuel technologies are to ours. Further, other scientific advances were calling for faster and more efficient methods of performing large computations.

In the early 1820s, Babbage came up with an idea for a machine that would automatically compute log tables. He received financial assistance from the British government to build his "Difference Engine," but, as in Leibniz's case, contemporary craftsmanship and machine technology were not sophisticated enough to produce a machine capable of the precise calculations Babbage envisioned. He eventually gave up work on the Difference Engine.

In spite of an intermittent nervous breakdown, Babbage plowed on, and by the 1830s he had conceived—and become obsessed with—his "Analytical Engine." It would run on gears, shafts, and ratchets, be driven by steam, and have a place for entering numbers as well as instructions for computing those numbers. It would have a place to carry out arithmetical operations (the "mill"), a storage area to hold subtotals and instructions for the whole operation (the "store"), and a register where the results would automatically appear after all the calculations had been completed—not terribly unlike a crude version of today's computer.

It was the instructions that were crucial. They defined the nature of the machine and constituted what we would call a computer program. What Babbage

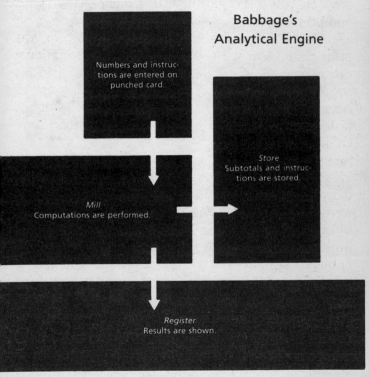

**Babbage's
Analytical Engine**

Numbers and instructions are entered on punched card.

Store
Subtotals and instructions are stored.

Mill
Computations are performed.

Register
Results are shown.

had designed was actually the first programmable computer. It was a revolutionary notion and was based on a technique that had been used in the French weaving industry since 1805.

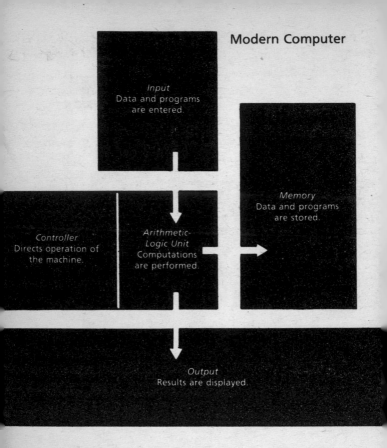

Modern Computer

Input
Data and programs are entered.

Memory
Data and programs are stored.

Controller
Directs operation of the machine.

Arithmetic-Logic Unit
Computations are performed.

Output
Results are displayed.

J.M. Jacquard was a Frenchman with a very good idea—a concept that many people are familiar with, since it is present in the workings of old player pianos. A continuous surface with holes punched in it arranged so they engage spokes, rods, or some other protruding device that controls the working of a machine, becomes a means by which the pattern of the machine's activities can be directed. One arrangement of holes causes one sequence of activities; another pattern produces a different result.

The weaving loom cards of J.M. Jacquard. The pattern in the cloth was determined by the pattern of holes on each successive card. The technique was employed again in the twentieth century in the IBM card.

In applying this idea to weaving, Jacquard directed (or programmed) the way threads were pulled through the loom, using a roll of punched cards for the loom movements. In a sense, these cards were the prototypes for today's IBM cards, except that Jacquard's cards were made of steel.

Babbage adapted these cards for his own machine. In the Analytical Engine they would serve to engage several of 80 studs; the pattern on the card would determine what number the studs were registering. By means of those numbers Babbage would feed to the machine, in numerical code, step-by-step instructions for computation, as well as the numbers to be computed. The computation would then be performed automatically. (Even in the first half of the nineteenth century the concept of automation was not unknown; some technology had already incorporated it in a small way. But it had never been used in computing numbers—that was revolutionary.)

A model of Charles Babbage's Analytical Engine.

And that was not the only new thing about Babbage's machine. The Analytical Engine would also be able to handle what were, in effect, forks in the mathematical road. It could be programmed to "choose" between alternate paths in a series of calculations. This would later be known as a "conditional branch," wherein the line of calculation branches off when a specific condition is met.

The Analytical Engine, however, was never built. Like the Difference Engine, it ran into problems of imprecise machinery and precise mathematics.

Babbage's eccentricities often made him hard to get along with, and he might have had a more difficult time attaining recognition for his work had he not had a devoted disciple in Augusta Ada, Countess Lovelace, daughter of the poet Lord Byron. A mathematician herself, Ada (for whom a computer language is named) publicized and championed Babbage's work.

Babbage grew bitter with age, having abandoned several major projects throughout his lifetime. When he died his brain was examined for possible physiological manifestations of his superior intelligence, but it proved to be a brain just like any other.

Into the Twentieth Century

Babbage's contributions, great as they were, were theoretical. Practical applications were the product of the fertile mind of Herman Hollerith.

Hollerith joined the U.S. Census Bureau during the tabulation of the 1880 census. The task of recording a population of fifty million was overwhelming the census takers, who in 1885 had yet to finish. Looking to the next count with dread, Census Bureau officials asked for ideas to quicken the process. Hollerith's were chosen, and in 1890 a census that some had feared would take at least seven years to be completed was effected in less than two months.

An 1890 cover of Scientific American *illustrates the use of Hollerith's punched cards in the processing of census data.*

Hollerith's solution was to use cards punched by hand and processed by electricity. They were placed over an electrically sensitive substance; when pins run over the cards came to a hole, they made contact with the conductor and completed a circuit, registering the information that had been coded in the pattern of holes on the card.

Herman H. Goldstine, in *The Computer from Pascal to von Neumann*, writes: "Hollerith realized that cards could be prepared by different people in different locations and at different times and then assembled in one large deck for subsequent tabulation; he also saw that cards could be sorted according to a given characteristic." With such flexibility, the system could be adapted to many types of information processing. Hollerith, fancying himself to be "the first statistical engineer," set up the Tabulating Machine

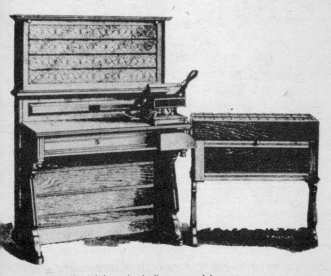

Photo courtesy of IBM Corporation

Herman Hollerith's tabulating machine.

Company in 1896. Railroads and insurance companie used his device to sort their records and other compa nies used them to keep better track of their sales. Hol lerith's firm was eventually merged with several other to form the Computing-Tabulating-Recording Compa ny, an ungainly name that was changed in 1924 to International Business Machines—IBM.

Punched card tabulators were refined furthe during the next few decades, as were mechanical of fice calculators, first produced on a mass scale by Bur roughs in the 1890s. (Until a few years ago these calculators were the most common means of calculat ing and sorting numerical data in all but the larges businesses.) But the demands of science and war related work necessitated machines of a higher orde —devices capable of handling long and complicated computations without the aid of a human operator a each step.

Advances in nuclear physics, especially, called fo more powerful machines. Vannevar Bush, an electrica engineer working at MIT in the early 1930s, devel oped an electronic machine that, like the slide rule, computed numbers by representing them in terms of something else. Where the slide rule used lengths of wood, Bush's differential analyzer (an analog device used to solve differential equations) employed varying voltages. (During World War II, Bush was named direc tor of the Office of Scientific Research and Develop ment.)

Alan Turing, a British mathematician, made a number of contributions to the development of the computer. The most basic was his theory that it was possible to build a general-purpose machine that could deal with any problem solvable by more specialized—or "dedicated"—computers. He also contributed some important theoretical work to the debate over whether or not the modern computer could emulate human thought. During World War II he worked on a number of machines built by the British government, and after the war he became director of the computing laboratory at the University of Manchester, where one of the most powerful machines of its time, the Manchester Automatic Digital Machine (MADAM), was built.

American Advances

In the late 1930s and early 1940s, two machines generally considered the immediate forerunners of the modern computer were constructed. The first was the brainchild of John V. Atanasoff, a physicist who envisioned his binary digit computer (more about binary digits later) while drinking alone on a cold winter's night in an Iowa bar. With a grant of $650, he and his assistant Clifford Berry put together the simple working model of an elementary computer.

In 1937, Harvard's Howard Aiken began to design another computer, for which he later managed to get financial support from IBM. Aiken had read Babbage, and admitted that if the Englishman "had lived seventy-five years later, I would have been out of a job." Aiken found himself a member of the U.S. Navy with the coming of the war, and it continued to supply financial support for the machine. In 1944 the Automatic Sequence Controlled Calculator (henceforth

The Mark I of the early 1940's. The action of its electrome-chanical relays, according to one observer, "sounded like a roomful of ladies knitting."

known as Mark I), an electromechanical machine with 760,000 parts and 500 miles of wire, was finally able to multiply two 10-digit numbers in less than 10 seconds. (A similar but smaller machine had been developed at about the same time at Bell Labs by George Stibitz.) Data was fed into the Mark I on punched paper tape and telephone-type relays were used to store the numbers. Science writer Jeremy Bernstein, then a Harvard student, remembers approaching the machine and hearing the "gentle clicking of the relays, which sounded like a roomful of ladies knitting."

Mark I was quite a sight. It took up a huge amount of space and the Navy engineers who ran it were so awed by it that they never really dropped their military demeanor. One observer commented that the

engineers seemed to be working "while at attention."

The next stage in the development of the computer was a crucial one. Before it could evolve to its modern state there had to be a breakthrough in the speed with which the machine could compute; groundwork had to be laid for a way to do this without continuously increasing the size of the machines until they became too large to use.

This modern computer would have two essential characteristics: it would be digital rather than analog, and it would count by 2s rather than the 10s we are accustomed to.

The digital computer was a significant step forward from the analog machine developed by Vannevar Bush. Analog machines measure something in terms of something else—in other words, by analogy. A thermometer, for example, is an analog device that represents degrees of temperature by a specific height of mercury in a glass tube. The slide rule is an analog computer that represents numbers by making their logs proportional to segments of a piece of wood.

A digital computer, on the other hand, deals with numbers directly, not by analogy. It doesn't measure: it counts. Instead of using physical objects that are proportional to quantities (which is far from mathematically precise), it uses some device to represent the numbers. The abacus, then, is a digital computer in which beads represent numbers. The first modern digital computers utilized electromechanical devices to count. To speed up the process, purely electronic devices were substituted: vacuum tubes were the first.

Decimal and Binary Systems

In order to follow the next step in the evolution of modern computers, we will need to take a brief side trip into the realm of numbering systems. When we count it is usually by 10s—the decimal numbering system. The abacus operates that way, but modern computers do not: because the decimal system uses the numbers 0 through 9, a machine based on that system would need devices to represent each digit in each column or place within a number. The number 237, for example, would require a sufficiently complex system to represent seven 1s, three 10s, and two

Decimal System	Binary System
0	0
1	1
2	10
3	11
4	100
5	101
6	110
7	111
8	1000
9	1001
10	1010
11	1011
12	1100
13	1101
14	1110
15	1111
16	10000

100s. A much larger number would require quite a bank of such devices.

One way to simplify matters is to use a system that counts by twos—the binary numbering system. Like the Morse code—a language constructed of only two symbols, the dot and the dash—the binary numbering system can carry out any computation possible in the decimal system by using just two numbers—0 and 1.

Whereas in the decimal system each column or "place" represents a power of ten—reading from right to left, ten to the zero (1s), ten to the first (10s), ten to the second (100s)—each place in the binary system represents a power of two—two to the zero (1s), two to the first (2s), two to the second (4s), two to the fourth (8s), etc.

The binary equivalent of 237, for example, would be 11101101. Numbers such as this can be added, subtracted, multiplied, and divided just like their decimal counterparts.

What's most important here is the ease with which a mechanical or electronic device can be used to represent 0s and 1s. A light bulb, for example, could stand for 0 if it were off and 1 if it were lit; a switch could represent 0 if open and 1 if closed. Anything that can exist in either one of two states, therefore, could be used by a computer to count with in the binary system.

So to the early computer scientists attempting to increase their machine's calculating speeds, a computer containing devices that could be switched back and forth quickly between two states—on and off, for example—would be a powerful machine capable of reaching calculating speeds never before attained.

Wartime Achievements

In the late 1930s, a young German engineer named Konrad Zuse—who claimed never to have heard of Babbage—built, in a corner of his parents' living room, the prototype of a machine which bore a close resemblance to the machine Babbage envisioned. It was a digital computer and may have been the first to use binary numbers. Zuse's computer stored numbers in common telephone relays, simple electromechanical switches that open or close by electrical current. Zuse later fed information to the improved version of this machine with punched 35mm film.

Although the machine was relatively primitive, it worked. It might have worked even better if Zuse could have taken the advice of a friend who suggested that vacuum tubes—scarce during the war—replace the relays. In 1940, Zuse offered his machine to the government of the Third Reich. But the German government thought the war's end was only a year away and was not interested in projects whose development could take longer. Later in the war a small version of the machine was used for designing aircraft, but by then the Germans were hopelessly behind in computer technology, enough to insure that they would never design the first functioning all-purpose computer.

During World War II, the British pursued the idea of a computer dedicated to just one purpose. Their Colossus project—building on the ideas of Alan Turing—used small, limited computers and enabled them to crack the German code.

The U.S. Army decided that it, too, needed a faster and more reliable machine than the Bush analog computer it was using to calculate tables of artillery trajectories.

In 1943, John Mauchly and J. Presper Eckert of the University of Pennsylvania, who were familiar with Atanasoff's work, began to build a machine on the same principles (this was later the subject of a lawsuit).

Their Army-financed machine was called the Electronic Numerical Integrator and Calculator, or ENIAC. It was the first general-purpose electronic digital computer. The "electronic" is important: their machine used vacuum tubes as on-off switches to store the numbers, but because it ran on the decimal rather than the binary system it needed ten tubes for every column.

For the first time a computer had been built in which there were, essentially, no moving parts. It could multiply two 10-digit numbers in three one-thousandths of a second. It had 18,000 vacuum tubes, weighed 30 tons, measured 10 feet high, 3 feet wide, and 100 feet long—and broke down every other day from the heat its 18,000 tubes generated. ENIAC made its debut in 1946, but it was obsolete the day it was turned on.

von Neumann

Early computers had to be partially rewired each time a different type of problem was to be solved. This was cumbersome and limited the usefulness of these early machines.

This problem was very much on the mind of John von Neumann in the mid-1940s. This Hungarian-born mathematician was already involved in calculations that would lead to the development of the hydrogen bomb. A brilliant thinker, he also had the ability to recall the specifics of anything he had ever taken the time to thoroughly reason out—not unlike a computer. His contributions to game theory had helped lay the groundwork for mathematical modeling (the simulation of real-life events by equations) and his vivid imagination was capable of seeing problems from new angles, even if they occasionally proved to be obtuse.

In a now-historic 1946 paper von Neumann published with colleagues Arthur W. Burks and Herman H. Goldstine, "Preliminary Discussion of the Logical Design of an Electronic Computing Instrument," the co-authors said that:

> the machine must be capable of storing in some manner not only the digital information needed in a given computation . . . and also the intermediate results of the computation . . . but also the instructions which govern the actual routine to be performed on the numerical data. In a special-purpose machine these instructions are an integral part of the device and constitute a part of its design structure. For an all-purpose machine it must be possible to instruct the device to carry out any computation whatsoever that can be formulated in numerical terms.

In other words, the program that was going to tell the computer how to handle the numbers being entered had to go into the machine at the same time and in the same form as the numbers themselves—this was the concept of the stored program. (Although this may seem obvious to today's computer operators, it was far from obvious in 1946.) The program would have to be entered symbolically (in code) rather than physically (by rewiring the machine for each different program).

Von Neumann's work on computers was spurred on by the need for better methods of calculating for the development of atomic weapons. He later joined the Institute for Advanced Studies at Princeton along with J. Robert Oppenheimer and other pioneers of atomic weaponry. In 1945 von Neumann wrote the first computer program instructions that directed a machine to put in numerical order a random list of numbers.

Von Neumann also anticipated the use of the program "loop," by which a computer can be programmed to continuously repeat a series of steps a given number of times. All of this would be done automatically, once program and data were entered into the machine.

Von Neumann's work transformed the computer. Stored programs became an essential part of all machines, such as EDSAC (Electronic Delay Storage Automatic Computer) and EDVAC (Electronic Discrete Variable Automatic Computer), which followed in the late 1940s.

UNIVAC—of which we have spoken already—the first universal, all-purpose computer, was developed by Mauchley and Eckert after they left the ENIAC project. Working in a Philadelphia building which bordered on a cemetery and a junkyard, they built the first "commercial" machine. Until this point computers had been government projects built to handle the computation of large numbers in defense-related work. When they entered the marketplace, the era of data processing began.

CHAPTER 3

FROM PUNCHED CARD TO KEYBOARD

The ability of the computer to store data and run programs computing that data without human intervention, as well as to make a choice based on the result of previous calculations, distinguishes it from the calculator. For example, we can write a brief program to make the computer print out a table of the U.S. dollar equivalent of French francs as long as we know the franc equivalent of one dollar. That program can be written and entered into the machine in a few minutes. It automatically runs at the push of a button, and it will work for as many different dollar values as we specify—1,000, for example. Using a calculator, we would have to calculate individually the franc equivalent of each dollar value: 1,000 separate calculations.

The computer is capable of making simple logical choices. What if we were in Paris, unfamiliar with the currency, and had limited cash but still wanted to go on a shopping spree? We could feed into a computer the prices, in francs, of all the things we wanted to buy, and then instruct the machine to start converting the values into dollars and add them up, item by item, until the total reached the limit of our funds. The program would tell the machine that after each item had been added to the total, the computer should check to see if our limit had been exceeded. If the total fell short of our limit, the computer would add on another item, check again, and so on until the limit was reached. At that point the machine would stop and tell us we had gone as far as we could go.

Of Bits and Bytes

Both data and programs are entered into the computer in the same way—in the 1s and 0s of the binary system. These binary digits have become known as "bits." Bits, like the dots and dashes of the Morse code, are combined into larger units to represent specific numbers, letters, and symbols.

These groups of bits (usually eight) are called "bytes." Most of the personal computers that have proliferated in the past few years use the 8-bit byte. (Let it not be said that computer people have no sense of humor; the 4-bit byte used in pocket calculators is called a "nibble.")

EBCDIC Representation of Capital Letters and Decimal Numbers

Character	EBCDIC	Character	EBCDIC
A	1100 0001	S	1110 0010
B	1100 0010	T	1110 0011
C	1100 0011	U	1110 0100
D	1100 0100	V	1110 0101
E	1100 0101	W	1110 0110
F	1100 0110	X	1110 0111
G	1100 0111	Y	1110 1000
H	1100 1000	Z	1110 1001
I	1100 1001	0	1111 0000
J	1101 0001	1	1111 0001
K	1101 0010	2	1111 0010
L	1101 0011	3	1111 0011
M	1101 0100	4	1111 0100
N	1101 0101	5	1111 0101
O	1101 0110	6	1111 0110
P	1101 0111	7	1111 0111
Q	1101 1000	8	1111 1000
R	1101 1001	9	1111 1001

The largest number of bits handled at any one time and stored in one place in the computer's memory is called a "word." Large computers handle words that are upward of 64 bits. This enables them to work faster and store more information than computers with smaller word capacities.

The way that alphanumeric characters (numbers, letters, and symbols) are represented in the machine has been standardized throughout the computer industry. The two most widely used of these "Morse codes" of the computer are ASCII (American Standard Code for Information Interchange) and EBCDIC (Extended Binary Coded Decimal Interchange Code), IBM's own code.

A "first generation" computer of the early 1950s.

Photo courtesy of IBM Corporation

Throughout the 1950s computer use grew slowly. The machines were still large, and very expensive. They continued to use vacuum tubes, although in fewer numbers. Programs had to be written out in the 0s and 1s that the machines recognized, which meant that they were very difficult to write and very easy to foul up. (The 1s and 0s formed numbers that were often 20 or 30 digits long.)

Mnemonic (memory) representation techniques were developed for those parts of the programs that told the machine what to do with the numbers. A long series of numbers, for example, could be summarized by just a few letters. Greater flexibility was also achieved with the development of the first programming languages. These refined codes not only abbreviated the symbolic expression of instructions, but they also eliminated the need to specify a memory location for every number entered (a requirement when using machine language); this was now done automatically. Later programming languages that resembled human language were adapted according to specific needs: FORTRAN and ALGOL, for example, were created for mathematical calculations; COBOL was developed for business use.

Although vacuum tubes continued to be the electronic means by which the 1s and 0s were registered until the late 1950s, other technologies such as magnetic cores passed in and out of vogue. These cores, for example, looked like miniature doughnuts with wires running through them. A current was passed through one of the wires, polarizing the magnets, and another wire read the polarization as either a 1 or a 0.

Transistors

A product bearing the now-familiar "solid state" designation does not run on vacuum tubes. Instead it uses the transistor, an invention that emerged from the Bell Telephone Labs in 1948. The transistor had several advantages over the vacuum tube: because it did not generate large amounts of heat it lasted almost indefinitely; it consumed less power; it was considerably smaller; and it was cheaper.

The transistor is a semiconductor, which means that it is only a fair-to-middling conductor of electrical current. It therefore makes a good switch: it can be swung either way with little outside help. It's a crystal, usually made from either silicon or germanium.

Smaller Is Better

Before the late 1960s, computers were found only in large institutions, and even they had only one big one. Various departments could use it, but only in turn.

But by the mid-1960s, integrated circuits (ICs) could hold thousands of transistors etched onto a silicon chip smaller than a postage stamp. The behemoth of the previous twenty years had now been domesticated. Digital Equipment Corporation produced a minicomputer in 1965 that sold for the bargain price of eighteen thousand dollars, enabling small companies and departments of larger companies to have their own machines. Big computers were now called "mainframes" to distinguish them from the smaller units.

IBM, which had not entered the computer market until 1954 (with its model 650), now introduced its model 360 family of computers, which set the standard for the industry in the 1960s. These computers were modular: all kinds of peripheral devices could simply be plugged into them. Their modularity had a

Smaller is better. The evolution of electronic circuits: vacuum tubes, transistors, integrated circuits, and very large scale integration.

profound influence on the future design and manufacture of computer equipment. Their popularity induced other manufacturers to make equipment that was "plug-compatible" with IBM machines, a procedure that is still popular today because it enhances the marketability of other manufacturers' products.

Miniaturization increasingly brought decentralization. More and more, computers were used "on line"—that is, operators interacted with them directly, feeding in data and queries on their own terminals (input and display devices that can be remote, and which were replacing the punched card systems), and getting almost instantaneous answers. Increasingly the computer was used to store and retrieve vast amounts of business information; it was not just for computing numerical problems any longer. Terminals continued to be placed at greater distances from where data was actually stored, and sophisticated telecommunication networks were being set up to facilitate long-distance data exchanges.

Transistors were reduced in size to the point where many thousands more could be crammed onto a tiny silicon chip. As transistors were made even smaller, the technology was referred to as large scale integration and, next, very large scale integration.

In 1971, the Intel Corporation introduced the "microprocessor" (Texas Instruments was producing it at about the same time)—the "computer on a chip." The 2,250 transistors packed onto this 1/6-inch by 1/8-inch chip had much more computing power than the lumbering ENIAC. These tiny and increasingly cheaper devices could do an array of things from powering a hand-held calculator to regulating the timing sequence of a washing machine.

By 1977 the microprocessor was a common part of many new American appliances. "Solid state" was no longer the last word; now it was "microprocessor-controlled." Hundreds of new products flooded the market thanks to this mighty element. *Fortune* magazine described the microprocessor as "one of those rare innovations that at the same time reduces the cost of manufacturing *and* enhances both the capabilities and value of the product."

The Computer Is Everywhere

At one time only Harvard or the U.S. government could have a computer; in the late 1970s computers became "personal." Children began to work with them in the early grades. Something called BASIC was becoming the most popular "foreign" language studied. And although the first personal computers appeared in the mid-70s it was not until 1981 that they really became familiar; by 1990 they may be as common a fixture as a television set.

The big machines have continued to get faster, and their ability to store information in a smaller space has increased. In the past few years the difference between the microcomputer (usually based on a single microprocessor) and the minicomputer has faded, as many businesses have opted for the more powerful and expensive microcomputer models. The distinction between minicomputers and mainframes has also begun to grow less clear. In 1982, Intel came up with the "micromainframe"—mainframe in its capabilities, and micro in size—the whole machine no larger than a telephone book.

There are still some computers that no one would mistake for ordinary machines—these are the very expensive supercomputers. Stripped-down versions of the Cray-1 and the Cyber 205, for example, can be had for a mere $10 million each. You wouldn't pick one up to teach yourself BASIC or to help your child with schoolwork, but they are good for solving advanced physics problems or the many equations used in weather forecasting. With a little arithmetic legerdemain, they can handle numbers as large as $10^{2,466}$. Their calculations are correct to fifteen decimal places to assure the accuracy of the final answer in a long series of computations.

Where Do We Go From Here?

The Cray-1 can perform an addition in 12 nanoseconds (billionths of a second). Even with solid state devices, such a calculation generates a lot of heat within the Cray-1's closely packed elements, so it has special cooling systems to prevent it from melting.

Very large scale integration methods can now pack as many as 100,000 components on a single powerful chip. One problem with reduced-size chips is that as they approach the micron size (.000039 inches), the electric charges on their memory switches are weaker: cosmic rays or normal background radiation from nearby objects such as the chip housing itself could be enough to alter the electrical charge, changing a 1 to 0, for example. And, the wavelength of the light soon will be too large: the chisel will be too big for the sculpture. In the near future X-rays will probably be used for this because of their shorter wavelength.

The downward limits of miniaturization for the integrated silicon chip are likely to be reached in the

1990s. Several ways of improving the chip's speed and memory capacity are currently being studied. Truly accurate weather forecasting is a task that requires these improvements. It involves trillions of calculations—what computer people call "number crunching." To perform such calculations silicon chips will have to be modified in some basic way or else be replaced by something else. Those presently used are not capable of attaining such calculating speeds. Chips installed in parallel circuits, capable of handling many calculations simultaneously, are now under development. They should be able to perform 6 billion additions per second, although they may prove difficult to program.

A replacement for silicon in some applications may be a man-made crystal fabricated by a new technique called "molecular beam epitaxy." This new crystal will probably be made from materials like gallium arsenide and be constructed one atomic layer at a time to allow complete control over its properties. "It makes you think you're in the next century," says one engineer who specializes in the field. Yet such advances are already underway at Bell Labs, IBM, and other institutions. This technique costs more than silicon and does not have the wide application of the older technology, but it may, on the other hand, allow for computing speeds four times as fast.

The speed of the current in a computer's circuits can be increased if resistance is lowered. When the temperature of metal approaches -450°F (absolute zero), it is no longer resistant to electricity and it becomes a superconductor. This concept is embodied in the Josephson junction, an electronic circuit that operates at very low temperatures. Experimenters at IBM are now immersing these circuits in liquid helium to bring them to a temperature near absolute zero. Computers utilizing this technology should be available in the near future.

Still another way of getting around the limitations of electric current is to replace electricity with light. Some materials either allow light to pass through them or will block it out, depending on whether or not another beam of light strikes the material—for which another on-off switch is used. These switches are considerably faster than solid state devices, but they consume more power and are considerably bigger. They are, however, immune to the static that can cause trouble for transistors.

The final frontier may be the strangest of all. In the late 1950s, a science fiction film called *The Incredible Shrinking Man* told the story of a victim of fallout from an atomic bomb test. As he became smaller he found himself inhabiting several different universes. First his pet cat became his mortal enemy, then a spider; then objects as small as a drop of water took on great significance. As the film ended he was still shrinking and the audience was left with the impression that he would soon be no larger than a molecule.

The final memory device could be either a natural or a synthetic molecule that could exist in one of two states. The problem, however, would be connecting these molecules to the computer. A possible solution would be to utilize gene splitting (a technique that uses genetically "programmed" bacteria) to construct a kind of protein backbone on which these molecules could be assembled to make up specific circuits.

We have come a long way from the vacuum tubes used in ENIAC. We have traveled equally as far in making the computer accessible to almost everyone. From government and university laboratories it has moved right into children's toy boxes. Semisophisticated computers can even be bought in the same stores as televisions and radios. Computers are almost as likely to be found in the workplace as are typewriters. The computer has become one of the basic machines of our time for any number of reasons—more, certainly, than you could count on your fingers.

CHAPTER 4

HARDWARE:
INPUT, STORAGE,
AND OUTPUT

A computer is a system of interrelated components and it is a much simpler system than it might appear to be. Actually, this system consists of just a few basic parts: an input device (for entering information), storage devices (for long- and short-term memory requirements), a central processing unit (to do the work), and one or more output devices (to feed out information or answers to the problems the computer has solved).

These different parts are referred to as hardware and are not terribly unlike the wires, plugs, glass gadgets, and electrical connections found in a hardware store. These are the tangible parts of the computer system, the elements you can touch and see.

Even more important, though, is the software—the programs that instruct the computer to carry out specific operations based on the data fed into the machine. These are the instructions that breathe life into the computer parts, that make them hum. In a sense, hardware without software is like a brain without thoughts.

The Computer Resembles Your Stereo

You might be surprised to know that in its basic structure the computer resembles an object that you probably already have in your living room. Like a computer, it stores information, processes it, and transmits it back in a different form from that in which it originally existed. Or didn't you ever think of your stereo that way?

The information that you feed into your stereo is music and spoken words. (The record industry itself, in fact, is beginning to refer to this "information" as software.) It is stored in two types of memory devices, tapes and records, and is accessed by means of a tape deck or record player. You may also have a communications device through which to bring in sound stored elsewhere: your FM tuner, or radio. These various "information" sources are connected to a preamplifier/amplifier (a tuner housed with a preamp/amp is called a receiver) that processes the information fed into it and sends it to the speakers or headphones—thus giving back the "information" in a form that makes sense and is usable. You may even want to get up and dance to it.

So, to paraphrase an old song, you push certain buttons down, and the information flows round and round, and it comes out here. The computer's information is also stored on tape and disks, which, as it happens, bear a close resemblance to those used by a stereo system. As a matter of fact, home computers often make use of an ordinary cassette tape recorder, and the computer disk drive resembles a phonograph somewhat. Like a stereo, the computer may utilize information stored at some distant site. Where a stereo's long-distance accessing of information is done by radio, the computer's data may be bounced off a satellite, travel through the air as microwaves, arrive via coaxial cable (many wires wrapped around each other, and capable of transmitting large amounts of information), or come through as prosaic a device

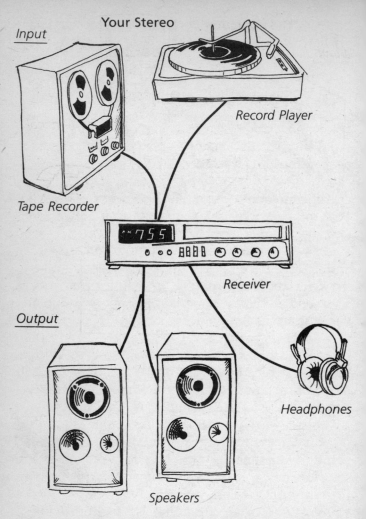

Your Stereo

Input

Tape Recorder

Record Player

Receiver

Output

Headphones

Speakers

as the telephone. (Sending information, computer-generated or otherwise, over long distances in this way is called telecommunications.)

The computer does employ one method of entering information for which there is often no parallel in a

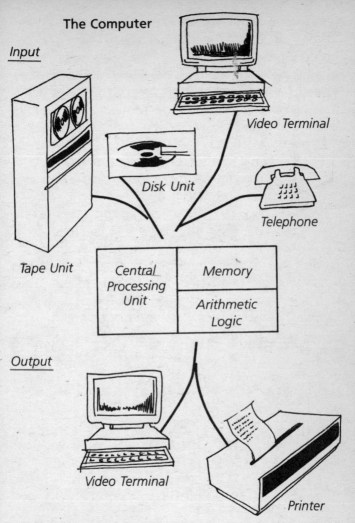

The Computer

Input

Video Terminal

Disk Unit

Telephone

Tape Unit

Central Processing Unit	Memory
	Arithmetic Logic

Output

Video Terminal

Printer

stereo unless the music system can connect a microphone directly to the receiver for recording purposes: information can be entered directly into a computer by typing it on a typewriterlike keyboard.

Just as the receiver is the heart of the stereo, so

the computer's most vital element is its central processing unit (CPU). Because of the receiver you can choose tape, records, or radio; you can raise or lower the volume and alter the tone of the music. Similarly, the computer's CPU controls the various input methods. Since it processes numbers rather than sound, it has an arithmetic section where computations can be performed; so it may make decisions about these numbers, it has a logic unit. And because it must temporarily store programs and the numbers involved in its computations, it has a memory unit.

When you listen to your stereo you hear the music—its output—through speakers or headphones. A computer's output is either information you are requesting or solutions to problems it has solved; this output can be transmitted by a number of devices of which TV-type screens and printers (like typewriters, but usually without keys) are the most common.

Input

IBM Cards—
The Earliest Input Method

Has anybody asked you lately for some "input"? The computer is always asking for it and is idle without it.

At the beginning of the computer era, punched paper tape and plug-in circuit boards were used to enter data and programs. In short order that was dwarfed by the use of the IBM (Hollerith's) card. This mode of entry is still used for many applications, al-

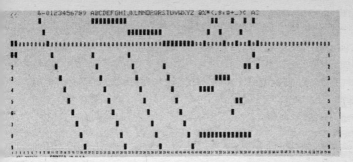

The IBM card.

though not nearly as many as fifteen to twenty years ago, when in most people's minds these cards symbolized the computer.

Punched cards come in more than one size, but the ones most often used contain 80 vertical columns and 12 horizontal rows of positions that can be punched to code information. The bottom nine rows are used to encode digits from 0 to 9. The three rows at the top are called zones. A letter is represented by a hole punched in one of the zone rows and a hole in one of the numerical rows. Symbols require two holes in the numerical area and one in the zone. All characters are entered according to a special card code named for Hollerith. Above each column, at the top of the card, the letter, number, or symbol encoded in the holes below it usually is printed out.

We are cautioned not to bend, fold, spindle, or mutilate these things because they have to be read and sorted by sensitive machines; a damaged card would gum up the works.

Information is encoded on cards by a keypunch operator at a machine with a typewriter like keyboard. Next the cards must be verified, again by machine, to make sure the holes have been put in the right places. Then the cards are fed into still another machine whose electrical sensors pick up the pattern of punched holes (at the rate of about 1,000 cards per minute) and feed this information to the computer's central processing unit, which stores the information in its memory in the form of 1s and 0s.

An IBM card can hold up to 80 bytes of information (one character in each of its 80 columns), a substantial amount for an object of this size. Cards are useful when speed is not of the essence and data must be available at every stage of processing and storage. The readable printed characters at the top of the card provide this accessibility.

One of the major uses of the IBM card today is in the billing process of utility and phone companies. The cards themselves are sent out as invoices. When a customer sends one back with a payment, the remittance is entered onto the card and it is fed back into the computer to update the company's records.

A keypunch operator codes information onto IBM cards.

CRTs

By the late 1960s, punched cards were being replaced by a quicker and more direct input method which also displays information: the computer terminal, also referred to as the cathode ray tube (CRT) terminal. Data is entered via a typewriterlike keyboard, the computer puts the data into its memory, and a message appears on the screen to verify the entry. (*New York Times* humorist Russell Baker once described this terminal as "a television set that rolls little, green, arthritic-looking letters and numbers across a dark screen," and added that he was still waiting for the commercial.)

Terminals are either "intelligent" or "dumb." A "dumb" terminal is passive; it simply receives and displays input information and does the same for the computer's response as output. An "intelligent" terminal, on the other hand, has a built-in microprocessor which allows the user to manipulate the data on the screen. The screen can be split, for example, to facilitate the comparison of two groups of figures or written text; the information on the screen can also be underlined and formatted in a variety of ways (type size or typeface, etc.).

Magnetic Ink and Optical Character Recognition

Another common input device is something that you encounter frequently but probably never think of as such. Take a look at the bottom left of the next check you write. The numbers there contain your account number and other information that the bank uses to route your check through the national banking system. The characters are printed in magnetic ink and can be machine read by means of an iron head which senses the magnetism in the ink. Many people never notice that when they get back their cancelled checks, another series of numbers have been added at the bottom right: the amount the check was written for. During the past thirty years the number of checks processed by American banks has gone from about 8 to over 30 billion a year. The ability to process this information automatically has kept the system from drowning in its own flood of paper.

The optical character recognition (OCR) method is similar to the magnetic ink process. Magnetic ink is not required because the computer can actually read characters printed in a special type style—the kind that somehow always looks as if it were written by and for a machine. A special device uses a beam of light to scan the shape of each character, and then compares it to letter and number shapes stored in the computer's memory. When it recognizes a shape as a specific character, that information is input into the computer. A credit card, for example, bears these special characters; after your charge slip is written up, it will be read by the OCR process.

MEMO _____

⊕⑆013201241⑆ ⑈4⑈024⑈057⑈

Magnetic ink characters at the bottom of a cancelled check.

A variation of optical character recognition allows many kinds of information to be fed to a computer automatically. If you've ever indicated test answers by filling in a skinny rectangular space with a pencil, you've prepared data for optical character recognition. A simple program tells the computer where the correct mark should be for each question and then the machine calculates your score.

Optical character recognition has lately come to play an increasingly large role in retail businesses. Did you ever wonder what those unevenly spaced series of black bars on prepackaged supermarket items were? If the store where you shop has already converted to Universal Product Code pricing, you probably have some notion. It's an optical character recognition code that identifies the product when the code is read by a small computer called a point-of-sale device, a machine that looks like a fancy cash register. The type and brand of item as well as its current price are stored in the computer's memory.

Some clever and useful things can be done with the help of this code. For example, let's say canned peas are on sale at three for a dollar. The clerk passes two cans over the sensor and then reaches for a different item. The peas are rung up at thirty-four cents per can, which is not three for a dollar. Should you be outraged? No—because when that third can shows up next to the hamburger meat and ice cream it will register as thirty-two cents. The computer didn't forget any more than you did.

Use of the bar code, of which the Universal Product Code is one variety, has been spreading to a wide range of fields. Scandinavian Airlines has begun to code its air cargo documents with the familiar black

The electronic cash register is the central part of the "point-of-sale device." When a memory unit and a scanning device are added, groceries bearing the Universal Product Code can be checked out without being manually rung up.

bars in order to facilitate handling. You may even see these bars imprinted in the back of library books. When you borrow one the library's computer automatically records the transaction; the librarian passes a wandlike device over the bars, by which the machine reads the code.

Graphic Input

In addition to alphanumeric form, data may be entered by means of computer graphics—charts, graphs, animation designs, and visual games. When a terminal screen is divided into a grid resembling graph paper, a limited number of points is produced where the vertical and horizontal lines meet. (Regular television screens offer fewer points and lower picture resolution than monitors built specifically for this purpose.) Information is plotted (entered) by identifying points and directing the computer to connect them to form whatever shapes your imagination can conjure up. To the computer, of course, they're just the coordinates for a series of dots (called "pixels"), but to you they're a picture.

Light Pens

Although graphic information can be entered on a keyboard, there are other more direct ways of doing it. A light pen containing a photoelectric cell is used in one method. Coordinates can be plotted on the screen by shining the light at specific points on the grid, thus "drawing pictures" on the screen that are then forwarded to the computer's memory. Another device, the digitizer, contains a pressure-sensitive writing surface connected to the computer. As you draw with a pen or pencil, the grid coordinates you pass over are entered into the machine's memory for processing. There are several variations on this method of entering grid coordinates; one even scans a drawing with lasers.

Light pens are also used for data entry, in what is perhaps the simplest method of all. The light pen is a "user-friendly" technique (easy for those unfamiliar with computers) that can be employed when the user is to choose from a variety of options displayed on the terminal screen. The user simply points at the desired choice with the light pen and the computer recognizes it as input. Some screens even feature a touch-sensitive display—you literally touch what you want.

Analog to Digital

Information from analog measurement devices can be fed into computers as input. In a steel mill, for example, if the temperature rises above a certain point, changes in the steel-making process might be called for. The temperature would be measured by an analog device and then "digitized"—changed by an analog-digital converter to 1s and 0s—by frequently sampling the information from the thermometer and assigning the changing analog values to predetermined digital levels. The computer can also be programmed to alter the production process itself whenever the temperature reaches a certain level. When information is entered and there is a computerized response in order to maintain a constant condition, the system works much like a thermostat. This process is called feedback.

Voice Recognition

Another input procedure borders on the truly fantastic. Although it is still in a primitive stage of development and its applications are limited, it offers much promise for the future. The quickest way to give a computer information would be to speak to it—if that were possible. It is, in fact, and the equipment to do it with has been commercially available since a company called Threshold introduced it in 1972. Voice recognition, as it is known, is especially useful in quality-control operations where workers' hands must be free to examine the product (a microphone is usually worn on a headband), as well as in other applications where material is handled, evaluated, and classified. Voice recognition is also used as a security device that permits entry only to those whose voices are recognized.

The computer digitizes the user's speech pattern and stores it in memory. That pattern is created by "training" the machine: each word in a limited vocabulary is spoken to the machine up to ten times. The computer then creates an average model of the sound of each word by measuring the variations in sound loudness, length, and pitch as each word is spoken. When the users are actually at work, the computer compares the sound of their voices with the pattern stored in its memory. (Workers must identify themselves beforehand so the right set of model sounds may be referred to.) The computer can then listen right through accents, hoarseness, and colds for basic speech patterns.

Data Storage

The two methods of long-term storage for computer data and programs are tape and disk. These media are used as off-line storage to hold information when the computer is turned off and its main memory is wiped clean. (They are also input devices.) Roughly speaking, they are the functional equivalent of those same components in a stereo system.

Magnetic Tape

Computer magnetic tape has been in use since the 1950s and is usually ½ inch wide by 1,800, 2,400, or 3,600 feet long. Bits are recorded at two fixed frequencies, one for 0s and the other for 1s. They are recorded 8 across, each on a separate parallel track, to make up 1 byte or character. One reel of tape can hold up to 150 million alphanumeric characters—as much information as several hundred thousand punched cards.

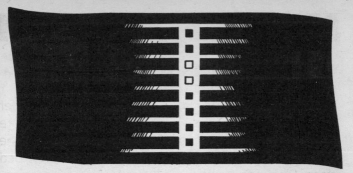

Computer Tape. To make up one byte (or character), bits are recorded in parallel, eight across, each on a separate track. This diagram shows how the binary number 3 would be stored as 1111 0011 in the EBCDIC code. The dark spaces each indicate a high frequency tone representing a 1; the two black spaces are the low tones, and stand for the two 0s in the binary number.

Disks

In recent years tape has been surpassed by disk as the most commonly used secondary storage medium (main memory is considered the primary storage system because although temporary it is in the machine itself). These disks spin considerably faster than records—2,400–3,600 revolutions per minute. Disks used in computer systems are made of aluminum or Mylar and hold millions of bytes (megabytes, abbreviated as ''M'') in concentric rings, within which the bits are stored magnetically in series, one bit following the next.

The Winchester disk (so named because IBM originally designated it as model #30-30, suggesting the rifle) is somewhat smaller than the large metal disk and is often used with personal computers in business applications. These disks are made of aluminum or hard plastic and are sealed to keep out dust. They hold up to 20 megabytes of data each.

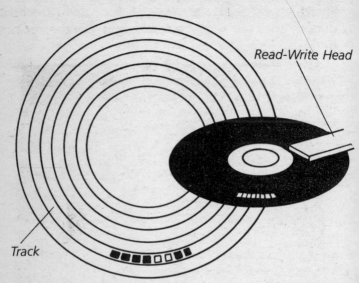

Read-Write Head

Track

Computer Disk. *The binary number 3 (1111 0011) as stored in series on a disk. The read-write head picks up the magnetic pattern and conveys it to the computer, where it is stored in the machine's main memory.*

Floppy Disks

The most widely used secondary storage medium for personal computers is the diskette made of Mylar, a plastic. Diskettes are three to eight inches in diameter, and because they are thin and supple they are often called floppy disks, or just "floppies." Each disk comes encased in a stiff paper jacket which should not be removed because the disk surface is easily contaminated by fingerprints and dirt, which makes it impossible to read. They hold less than one megabyte apiece, their particular capacity depending on how densely they are recorded upon and whether or not both sides are used.

Photo courtesy of IBM Corporation

A floppy diskette, the medium often used to store programs and data for use in personal computers.

Retrieving information from a disk is not unlike playing a record (although the "valleys" are pressed mechanically into a phonograph record, whereas computer disks are recorded magnetically). A reading-writing head containing a voltage sensor rides just above the metal disk (it slightly touches the

Mylar floppy). As it passes over the recorded track, the head reads the frequencies in the magnetized pattern. The computer converts this analog voltage measurement back into bits and stores it in its main memory.

Unlike your turntable, the disk drive can also record: it can transfer information from the volatile (erasable) main memory of the computer's central processing unit to the more permanent secondary storage of the disk.

To do this, the current in the reading-writing head magnetizes the disk to correspond to the pattern of bits in the information it is transferring.

Disk has one tremendous advantage over tape, and it relates to the very essence of the computer's efficiency—speed. If you want to retrieve information recorded in the middle of a reel of tape, you must run through the reel as quickly as the tape drive will allow until you reach the right spot. This process is called sequential access and it takes time—a precious commodity for a computer.

But it's a different story with the disk. You know that you can listen to any portion of a musical recording simply by picking up the tone arm and placing it down any place you wish: if there are seven songs on that side and you only want to hear the fourth, you can go right to it. The computer disk works the same way: if you type into your terminal a request for information stored in the middle of the disk, the computer directs the disk head to go right to the appropriate spot and retrieve the data. It doesn't have to go through everything else preceding it. You are able to access at random, directly, and almost instantaneously, to anything on the disk.

Memory Capacity

A computer may be described in terms such as "32K RAM" or "64K RAM." The numbers and letters refer to how many thousands (K = kilos) of bytes the computer's main memory can accommodate. (Actually it's an approximate figure: 1K equals 1,024 bytes.) "RAM" (random access memory) refers to the way information can be retrieved from the main memory—by random access. Each switch in the main memory holds one bit; these switches are grouped together in 8s (to make up one byte, representing a character) and are assigned a particular storage position in the memory. The contents of any of these positions can be accessed directly by the computer's central processing unit, just as they can from any part of a disk.

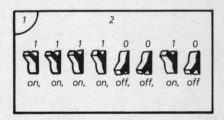

Eight bits, one byte representing the alphanumeric character "2" in memory.

Remember that RAM refers to a mode of access: direct rather than sequential. Technically, this term can—and does—apply not only to the main memory, but also to secondary storage devices such as disks. However, when a computer is said to have 64K RAM, the reference is made *only* to the storage capacity of the main memory. Storage provided for in secondary units would be additional.

How Information is Stored in the Main Memory

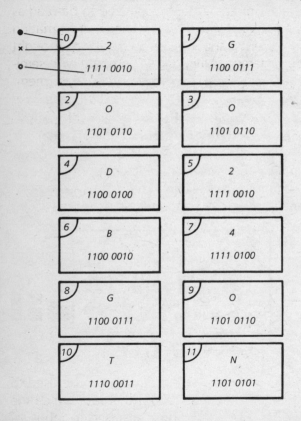

- *Address of Location in Memory*
- *Contents of that Location in Alphanumeric Characters*
- *Contents in EBCDIC Code*

Bubble Memory

New technologies are being explored for manufacturing both main memory and secondary storage units. A few years ago "bubble memories" were being touted as the technology of the future. In this case, specified recording spots on garnet film either are magnetized to indicate a 1 or are left unmagnetized to be read as 0. This is a nonvolatile device; it retains its information when the current is shut off. For a time it was thought that bubble memories might even compete with semiconductors for a place in the computer's main memory. Their high cost, however, has limited their use, although they are found in some portable computers.

Optical Disks

Optical storage disks, similar to the videodisks and stereo digital disks that are now entering the market, store bits by means of lasers which bore microscopic pits corresponding to bit patterns on the surface of a disk. These disks are durable and not erasable. Although not yet widely available, it is anticipated that they may hold as much as fifty times the amount of information stored on conventional disks.

Output

A number of different output devices can be used to display, print or otherwise record the data which the computer has processed. Some are used to input information as well: survey results, for example, could be recorded onto hundreds of punched cards for permanent storage; a video terminal provides an excellent temporary visual display of database information.

The results of mathematical computations might be written directly to (that is, recorded on) tape or disk for long- or short-term storage.

Printers

A convenient means of providing a permanent record of the computer's activities uses the printer—a widely used output device. Even if you've never worked with a computer, you've probably seen a computer print-out. It's that fan-folded green and white paper with the holes along the edges, imprinted with those strange boxy letters. The holes are for the pins in the tractor-feed mechanism that pulls the paper through the printer; the odd-looking letters are produced by a process called dot matrix.

Dot Matrix Printers

Impact printers, which use a strike-on typewriterlike method, are the most popular type. Usually they produce dot matrix characters. Wires moving perpendicularly to the paper surface strike a ribbon with their ends to reproduce a horizontal and vertical pattern of dots which defines each character. This printing method is quick and relatively inexpensive, but the characters are not as legible as those produced by a typewriter and they shouldn't be used in business correspondence—unless you want the recipient to know you have a computer.

Letter-Quality Printers

Letter-quality printers produce characters as legible as those made by a good typewriter. As a matter of fact,

IBM Selectrics have in the past been adapted, with the addition of an interface, for use as computer printers. The drawback is their relatively slow speed (15 characters per second; a rate of 200 per second is not unusual for a dot matrix machine) and a tendency to break down under printing loads they were not built to handle.

Most letter-quality printers these days use a daisy wheel, a small round object with "petals" (spokes) radiating out from the center. At the end of each petal is one character; a small hammer strikes the character against a ribbon to print it. Each wheel holds about 95 characters. The right one is brought up by the rapid turning of the wheel, which works somewhat similar to the operation of the "golf ball" element in an IBM Selectric typewriter.

High-Speed Printers

Advanced technologies have produced high printing speeds. In some machines the characters are mounted on rapidly moving chains or drums. Bidirectional printers, which print left to right and then, utilizing memory devices, index down as many lines as needed and print right to left, are now common. Non-impact mechanisms have also recently come to the fore: thermal printing, which produces characters on specially treated paper by heated wires; electrostatic printing by electrical charges, also on special paper; magnetic force, which uses belts and heated ink; and a process similar to xerography, capable of producing 4,000 lines per minute. Finally, laser printing approaches the production of 20,000 lines per minute (but at a cost of $300,000 per machine).

On the frontier of printing technology is the ink

jet printer. It shoots out droplets of ink (as many as 100,000 per second) that are deflected to form characters on paper.

Graphic Output

Much computer output is now produced in graphic form. The plotter, for example, is a device that permanently records pictorial output by moving a pen or pencil across the paper in a pattern prescribed by the computer. This can be accomplished in black and white or in color.

For large amounts of data that will be stored for a long time and yet must be accessible, there is computer output microfilm. Microfilm or microfiche is produced by photographing the video terminal screen. It would take fifty minutes of impact printing to store what this method can pick up in five minutes at one-thirtieth of the cost. While the photography is being done the computer can be programmed to catalog everything so the information may be retrieved easily in the future. Paper copies can be made quickly from the microfilm with a device called a reader-printer.

Artificial Speech

In our look at input methods we learned that it is possible to speak to computers. Computers have been speaking to us for some time, through a process called speech synthesis. Talking toys, safety systems that cry out when dangerous conditions exist, and appliances that tell you which button to push are becoming commonplace. The next time you dial a telephone number and get a recording telling you that the number has been changed, consider this: not only are you hearing a recording rather than a live person, but the recording may not have been made by a live person in the first place.

Artificial speech is generated in one of three ways. The most common is formant synthesis, a technology pioneered by Bell Telephone and Texas Instruments. This process involves an analog measurement that is converted to a digital count and then is converted back to analog for the actual output. The phonemes, or basic speech sounds, are combined into words by programming the computer with the rules for word formations. (We humans can produce over one hundred of these basic sounds, but we only use about fifty in our speech.) The digitized sounds are converted into varying voltages that drive a speaker that reproduces clear—although somewhat robotlike—speech.

Linear predictive coding, a process used in Texas Instruments' Speak and Spell educational devices, digitizes not only phonemes but also a model of the way we produce those sounds. Waveform digitization, the third method, involves sampling the sound source (which is a sample human speech that it mimics) for its amplitude (loudness) and frequency (pitch), and converting these to discrete 1s and 0s that are stored in the computer's memory for future reference.

CHAPTER 5

HARDWARE: THE CENTRAL PROCESSING UNIT

So far we've seen that there are many ways of getting information into a computer and many ways to retrieve it. We've also looked at some devices for storing information outside the central processing unit, in components that may also be used as input devices when data is transferred to the main memory. Now we reach the core of the matter: how does this information get from one end of the computer to the other, and what happens to it in between? What do those circuits inside actually do to make the computer a computer?

Computers are actually a lot like giant train-switching yards. Access to the yards (the central processing unit) must be carefully controlled (users must often identify themselves with the correct password). Most of the activity inside the yard involves moving trains around from tracks to sidings and back again (a lot of time is spent in setting up and manipulating data to prepare for the computation). Finally, a small portion of the work time is actually devoted to adding cars to one train and detaching them from another (the actual computation is performed).

The Controller

More than one input and secondary storage device can be connected to a central processing unit (CPU) at one time. (The central processing unit is the heart of the computer, where all the work is done. It's something like the engine in your car.) Some of these devices, such as disk and tape, have mechanical as well as electronic components and therefore relay information at varying speeds. At any one time there may be a good deal of traffic coming into the computer. Electronic representations of 1s and 0s will be traveling at speeds and arriving at intervals not necessarily to the computer's liking.

Bits must travel at an exact speed and with specific intervals between them for the central processing unit to perform its job correctly. This is all set straight within the circuit (or channel) in which information actually flows into the computer. Buffers receive the incoming traffic, put it "on hold," and then pass it on at the right speed and interval. In larger machines, a microprocessor (actually a small, second computer) is built into the channel to regulate input.

The controller, that part of the central processing unit which actually manages the activities of the computer, contains a program called an operating system, to link up with and control the various input and secondary storage devices. Thus the computer can direct a disk drive to turn on, move its head to a particular spot on the disk, and pull out some information and send it on to the computer's internal or main memory.

ROM and RAM

This operating system program is often stored in that part of the computer's memory known as the "read only memory," or ROM. It is distinguished from the main memory's random access memory (RAM) because, as its name says, it can be read only; it can never be erased and recorded on (well, almost never: some ROMs—"Erasable Programmable ROMs," or EPROMs—can be altered and thus the basic functioning of the computer changed, but it's an involved process).

RAM is volatile: when you turn off the current, whatever was in main memory disappears—data, programs, everything. ROM, on the other hand, is permanent and stable. RAM is temporary: it stores the data and programs needed to solve a particular problem. When that problem is solved, the memory will be cleared and either a new set of data with its program will be entered or the machine will be shut off. ROM manages and oversees the work of the computer: it contains the workaday programs originally built into the computer.

RAM holds the raw material from which the final product is made but ROM runs the factory. RAM is like a piece of scrap paper that is critical to your figuring or the creation of an important list, but something you can discard once the task is done; ROM is like an instruction manual that will be just as handy a month from now as at this moment.

Once in the computer, each byte of information is assigned to a particular memory location. Each of these locations is numbered; that number is referred to as the address of that position in memory. You might want to think of a 64K machine as having about 64,000 houses (65,536—or 1,024 × 64—to be exact), each with its own address. The contents of any one of these "houses" is a letter, number, or symbol in the form of a byte, which contains the 1s and 0s registered by the semiconductors at that location. The contents (information) should not be confused with the address.

The CPU Simplified

We seem to have gone into excruciating detail about how data and programs enter and are stored in the computer. But in a sense this systematic handling and setting up of the material that the computer will process demonstrates a vitally important aspect of the computer's mode of functioning: there is a place for every piece of data, every line in the program. Each specific action is carefully planned. If any one of these pieces is out of place, things simply don't go as they should.

There's nothing mysterious about the way computers actually operate on data when programs are run. If anything, the process may seem disappointingly simple, even clumsy. The whole process will be clearer if we look at an analogy.

Arithmetic/Logic Unit: Analogy

Let's say we want to run a program to add the numbers 15 and 14. Imagine several people in a room with two tables. On one table is a row of numbered shoe boxes, each of which will serve as memory locations. On the other table is a single box that will hold (or accumulate) the numbers to be added: it's called the accumulator. We are outside the room with two bags of marbles, one holding fifteen and the other four-teen. We've also written a short list of instructions (our program) which tells the people inside the computer room what we want done with our marbles.

When we're ready to run the program, we knock on the door; the person who will act as the input device comes out. We hand him the marbles and our instructions.

He brings them all into the room, which is the equivalent of the central processing unit. Standing at the center of the room is the controller, who will direct the whole operation. She takes the marbles and the instructions and is about to have them placed in the memory boxes when she realizes that the instructions are in German. She understands only English, so she takes out a German-English dictionary and translates the instructions.

She then assigns each of the instructions and pieces of data to a memory storage box. There are twenty boxes but she only needs the first four. Each instruction is tagged to indicate which box holds the next relevant piece of information in the program sequence. She turns to one of the many registers who act as her assistants and tells him to write down the number of the box that contains the first instruction, box #1.

Everything is ready to go, but with all this house-keeping activity and people moving about, it will be necessary to impose some order on things. Some-body—the timekeeper—will stand off to the side with a stopwatch and count off the seconds. People may move and perform their work only at the specific intervals when the timekeeper yells "move."

He does so, and the number one register announces that the first instruction is being called up. He gives the box number of this first instruction to another register, who walks over to the table, opens the first box and brings its contents back to the center of the room. The instructions say that the contents of memory box #2 should be placed in the accumulator box on the second table. Another register goes to memory box #2, opens it and finds fifteen marbles, which he takes to the other table and puts in the accumulator box, as instructed. It's all marvelously orderly.

The first assistant says that it is now time for the second instruction, which will be found in the third memory box. Those instructions are retrieved; they say that the contents of the fourth memory box should be added to whatever is already in the accumulator box on the other table. An obliging register goes to the fourth memory box, opens it, discovers fourteen marbles, and takes them over to the accumulator box. He adds them to the fifteen already there and announces that there is a grand total of twenty-nine. The controller then assigns another assistant to be an output. He exits the room with the number 29 written on a piece of paper and hands it to us. The program has been run and we have our answer.

This, you may be thinking, is "high tech?" This is sophistication? It almost sounds like we are dealing with a Rube Goldberg device—a whole factory just to add one bunch of things to another, and announce the result. Oversimplified and schematic though the analogy may be, this basically is it. And it does make sense. It may not represent the most aesthetically pleasing technology ever developed, but the process can be run millions of times a second and it gets the

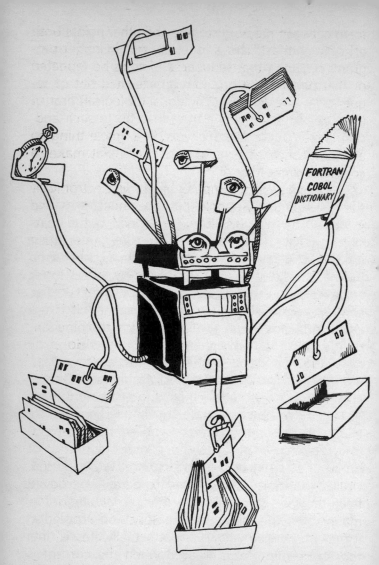

job done.

The configuration of the solid state devices used in a computer makes all of this movement back and forth between memory storage and other points both efficient and fast. This is especially true in longer programs requiring that sequences of steps be repeated or that parts of the program be executed out of sequence as a result of a conditional (or logical) branch ("if a certain condition is true, then go to such-and-such a step"). It is this ability to do a simple thing an almost inconceivable number of times that makes a computer what it is.

In real life, the computer performs electronically the tasks of those people with the shoe boxes and marbles. The computer also has a clock, but it beats out rather than records time. At regular intervals it emits electrical pulses which control the rhythm of the machine's operation; bigger machines have shorter intervals between beats and thus work faster. The computer must also translate the programs it is fed into a language it can understand—the machine language peculiar to that computer. This is done by means of a translating program within the computer.

An electronic counting register in the machine keeps track of the program to assure that everything is done in its proper order. Data and instructions are retrieved from memory locations as needed and temporarily stored in other registers until the computation or processing for which they are required is performed. Unlike the marbles, which were actually removed from the shoe boxes and left them empty, the information from the computer's memory is only copied so it may be worked with. It is not actually erased until the entire memory is cleared when the current is turned off. Arithmetic operations are carried out in the arithmetic/logic unit and the results are stored in the accumulator, which acts as a kind of electronic scratch pad. When the program has been run the final results are displayed on an output device.

The Logic Section

Up to now we've been looking at the functions of the arithmetic/logic unit within the CPU without paying much attention to the logic section. The logic circuits make comparisons between two quantities to see if one is less than, more than, or equal to the other, and then makes "decisions" based on these comparisons—the step we alluded to earlier that seemed to border on "thinking."

This process may be thought of as an electronic expression of the concepts of Boolean algebra, which was developed by George Boole, a contemporary of Charles Babbage. Boole's system expresses logical propositions in simple algebraic terms using just two values, true and false. Modern computer builders using a two-value system of 1s and 0s employed Boole's system in computer circuits designed to express logic in terms of those numbers. These circuits enable computers to recognize if one number is less than, equal to, or greater than another number.

Lewis Carroll's Tweedledee once observed that "if it was so, it might be; and if it were so, it would be, but as it isn't, it ain't. That's logic." Actually, *that's* entertainment—logic is more mundane.

Let's say that a big company is taking inventory (an onerous task) and it wants to reward with a bonus every employee who puts in at least thirty hours of overtime in the two weeks it takes to count every widget in the warehouse. The programmer has inserted into the payroll program a step instructing the computer to check the number of overtime hours each employee has worked. If the total exceeds 30, that worker's records are run through a special part of the program that will add twenty-five dollars to his paycheck. (For this he gave up bowling?)

If John Doe worked fifteen hours of overtime the first week and fourteen the second, how does the computer know that he missed the bonus by sixty minutes? Simply by subtracting the number of overtime hours he worked from thirty. If the result is a negative number or 0, he's eligible for the bonus. Otherwise Mr. Doe's records will proceed through the program sequence without special treatment. It's not thinking at all—just some simple arithmetic and a sorting routine. The computer made a comparison between two numbers, and based on the outcome of the comparison, acted accordingly. The real thinking was done by the programmer who instructed the machine to treat the data in this manner.

CHAPTER 6

SOFTWARE:
IT'S PROGRAMMED
FOR ACTION

A recent issue of the *New Yorker* carried a cartoon depicting the front of Schwartz's Hardware Store. Middle-aged Mr. Schwartz, slouch-shouldered, his face emotionless, stands in the doorway next to the window sign advertising electrical and plumbing supplies. His young employee is parting with these words: "So long, Mr. Schwartz. I'm leaving. Nowadays, software's where it's at."

Whether or not you appreciate the humor, the cartoon does make two valid points about computers. First, computer terminology has become so familiar to the general public that the cartoonist could assume that the double meaning of "hardware" would not be lost—and yet not so familiar that the pun wouldn't startle for a second, and then cause some amusement. Second, software *is* where it's at.

When the computer era was in its infancy, four times as much was spent on hardware as on software or programming. That ratio has now been reversed. Computer manufacturers spend vast sums to have long and intricate programs written for their machines. Design engineering has now taken a back seat to devising complex systems of instructions to put the machine through its paces.

Companies and individuals who buy computers are investing a good deal of money in software, or applications programs—the sets of instructions that tell the machine how to deal with specific jobs and problems. Large companies tend to have their own highly paid staff of systems analysts, who evaluate the company's data processing needs and break the work down into logical steps, and programmers, who take that logical design, code it into the appropriate computer language, and write the program.

There is also a great demand for prewritten programs that have general applicability and can be adapted to any business (or household) need such as bookkeeping or sales forecasting routines. And sometimes a service company with a large staff of analysts and programmers will be hired to custom design a program for a smaller business.

What's in a Program?

The program defines what kind of machine the computer is at any given moment. If you are running a program to compare the relative value of various kinds of bank certificates at different interest rates and maturities, the machine is serving as a sophisticated automatic calculator. If you are using it to search through a long list of names randomly arranged and print out in alphabetical order all those beginning with the letters A through G, it's a machine that compares, sorts, and retrieves information. The computer is one of the most versatile machines ever built; its programs make it so.

Mathematicians refer to the procedure for solving a problem as an algorithm. That's what a program is, whether it's dealing with a mathematical problem or not. It's written in explicit, logical order and everything is spelled out clearly. For example, if we wrote a program for adding the two-place decimal numbers 15 and 14, it would look something like this:

1. Write down the numbers so that one is directly under the other.

2. Add the numbers in the units column.

3. If the sum of the numbers in the units column is *less* than 10, write it down and proceed to the next column.

4. If the sum of the numbers in the units column is equal to or *more* than 10, enter the units figure in the units column; carry the other digit to the next place.

5. Add the numbers in the second column, including anything carried over from the first column; write this number down.

6. Stop.

In other words:
$$15 \\ + \underline{14} \\ 29.$$

The program we used was a general one, applicable to the addition of any two-digit decimal numbers. The data we used were the numbers 15 and 14.

In a sense, we use algorithms—problem-solving methods involving the repetition of one or more procedures—to accomplish almost everything we do from the time we get up in the morning until we fall asleep at night; we just don't think about it that way. We do face some problems, however, that we must carefully and consciously reason out in order to work through from one end to the other. One recurring example—which itself very much resembles a computer program and in fact can be dealt with by computer—

is that annual government document for which we must supply data, perform various operations on that data, and put in the mail by midnight on April 15th each year.

Example: IRS Form 1040

IRS Form 1040 provides step-by-step instructions on how to complete the process, from entering your name and address to computing your final tax liability. In between it calls for unknown quantities (known as variables in computer programs) such as "adjusted gross income." Each specific category was designed into the tax form, but *you* must fill in the blank space with the correct data; you must indicate what "adjusted gross income" equals when you run this "program."

Like some computer programs, Form 1040 has conditional branches. Should you itemize? Fill out Schedule A and see if your final figure exceeds the standard deduction. If it doesn't, take the standard deduction and proceed to the next line.

In writing computer programs, logic is all. The program must draw you inexorably from the first step to the last. Everything must be dealt with in sensible order. Remember the King's advice to the White Rabbit, who was about to testify at the trial in *Alice in Wonderland*: "Begin at the beginning . . . and go on till you come to the end: then stop."

Before writing anything of length and complexity, it's wise to make an outline. The same rule applies when writing a computer program, whose outline is even more detailed than that which is required for prose writing.

Flowcharts

The most commonly used outlines are called flow-charts. You may have seen similar charts in other contexts. If, for example, you took high school civics or an introductory college course in government, you can probably recall a chart that demonstrated the step-by-step procedure for getting a bill through Congress. Or, if you work for a large company, the executives in your firm probably consult flowcharts that show in systematic detail the procedures for running each department and the way those departments interact with each other.

A computer flowchart is the model from which the actual program is written, in the computer's language. When computer flowcharts are prepared, certain conventions are followed pertaining to the shape of each of the geometric figures that contain the program's successive steps. For example, the conditional branch step is represented by a diamond, as you can see in the accompanying diagram which outlines the method of deciding whether or not to itemize on your income tax return.

The computer, when running the program, begins with the program steps at the top of the flow-chart. If the condition of the branch is satisfied—that is, if the Schedule A total is greater than a zero—the computer follows the directions that appear off to the side of the diagram before it returns to the main line of the program. If the condition is not satisfied—if it

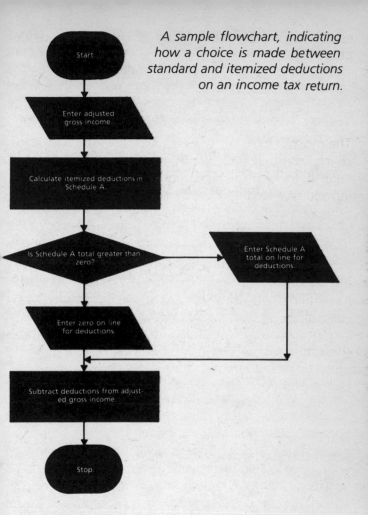

A sample flowchart, indicating how a choice is made between standard and itemized deductions on an income tax return.

turns out that you don't have enough deductions to make it worthwhile to itemize—then the program continues to run straight out through the bottom of the diamond and down the line until it reaches the end.

This, of course, is only a part of what you might

have to go through to compute your income tax. A program for handling the whole return would be considerably longer and more complicated, although it would have to be more clear and precise than Form 1040 itself. Once this program is written, it can be stored on disk or tape and transferred into the computer whenever it is needed.

Prompt statements (or input statements) can be inserted into the program to generate a series of questions on the terminal screen, so the machine can elicit from you the data it needs to compute your taxes. In this particular program, for example, the computer would ask you to type in your medical expenses, mortgage interest, real estate taxes, etc. Then, to calculate your total itemized deductions, it would perform all the necessary computations based on formulas that had been taken from the tax instructions and written into the program.

Programs need not last forever. One created to do your taxes would be obsolete as soon as the tax law changed. Most likely a business program written twenty years ago was not designed with future hardware improvements in mind. And, if the company had grown substantially, the program might no longer be able to deal efficiently with vastly increased quantities of data. Writing some new programs can take hundreds of man years and cost a good deal of money, so it often seems cheaper to have programs updated than completely rewritten. But while the programmers are tinkering, business must go on, all the while using a computer system that is becoming more and more obsolete. "It's like being down in the swamp fighting alligators," one harassed executive recently observed. "You can't figure out how to drain the swamp to escape, because the alligators keep coming at you."

Talking to Transistors

Programs must be coded in a specific form, or language, in order to be fed as input to the computer. Early programmers were confined to a language of 1s and 0s: they wrote programs in a form that could be used directly by the machine. These programmers had to specify everything, every step of the way. They had to keep track of the memory address of every piece of data entered, for example, spelling out exactly where each item was being moved to every time it was shifted around within the machine. If you recall from the marbles-and-shoe-boxes analogy how much moving around has to happen to perform a simple addition, you will understand the magnitude of their task.

Machine Language

When you see just what a step in this kind of program would have looked like you are bound to have an even more vivid impression of the travails of the first programmers. As we have already learned, every computer model has its own operation code, or particular combination of 1s and 0s to represent the operations being carried out. That is the machine language of that particular model of computer. In machine language, a typical instruction for a large machine whose memory locations are each capable of holding 12 bits of information (4 bytes) might look like this:

1010010000111001101001010011010

The first 8 bits would be the operation code: let's say that to this computer it means "add." The next 4 bits signify a register—a temporary storage location—and the final 20 are the address of a specific memory location. The computer is being told to take the contents of that memory location and add it to register #1.

This is just one line out of possibly hundreds or thousands. It's amazing that the first programmers did not go blind—or insane.

Early on, attempts were made to simplify machine language. The long instruction numbers were shortened by expressing them in a numbering system based on 16 (hexadecimal), which uses digits 0 through 9 and letters A through F to create figures as high as 16 in any column or place. (That large number above, for example, would be A439A53A in hexadecimal.) In this improved system each machine language number was only one-fourth as long as it had been originally. But it was still a number and meant little to anyone but the person who had actually written the program.

Assembly Language

The development of brief symbolic abbreviations for operation codes and the use of symbolic names to describe the contents of a memory location were major breakthroughs which rescued programmers from the morass of machine language. If, for example, that 32-

digit binary monstrosity had been part of a payroll program, it might have been written in the new method as:

Add 3, OT

—meaning, "Add overtime hours" (the contents of the memory location to be found at that 20-digit address) "to register #3."

Assembly language, the name for this vastly improved coding method, had several advantages over machine language. Obviously, it was shorter. It was also easier to read because operations were literally spelled out. And the programmer no longer had to specify where each variable in a program would be stored because the computer was now able to do it automatically.

High-Level Languages

Unfortunately, assembly language programs take a long time to write and are not very comprehensible to people who have only a limited background in computers. Computer professionals realized that if these machines were to come into general use, higher-level languages, closer to human languages, would have to be developed. The number of lines in the program would have to be shortened and the machine itself

The Ascent of Programming Languages

English? Perhaps in the future.

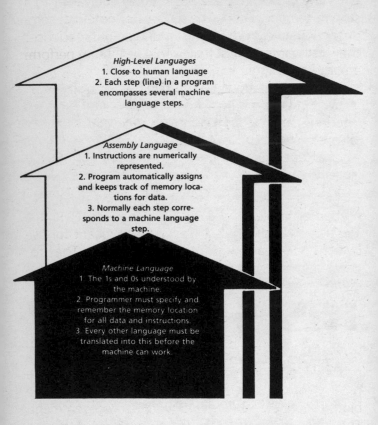

High-Level Languages
1. Close to human language
2. Each step (line) in a program encompasses several machine language steps.

Assembly Language
1. Instructions are numerically represented.
2. Program automatically assigns and keeps track of memory locations for data.
3. Normally each step corresponds to a machine language step.

Machine Language
1. The 1s and 0s understood by the machine.
2. Programmer must specify and remember the memory location for all data and instructions.
3. Every other language must be translated into this before the machine can work.

would have to keep track of where information is stored throughout the CPU, and the like. The programming burden would have to be lightened so that each line in the program was roughly equivalent to a step in the flow chart. The millions of potential computer users were not interested in computer science: they just wanted a tool that would help them perform a specific job more easily.

FORTRAN

The first important high-level language was developed by IBM in the mid-1950s. At this point computer use was still weighted heavily towards dealing with numerical problems, and this new language, FORmula TRANslator (or FORTRAN), was initially meant for use by mathematicians, scientists, and engineers. The program that translated FORTRAN instructions into machine language—the first compiler program—contained about 25,000 lines and cost IBM about $2.5 million to develop.

By the late 1950s demand was building for a language that would be more suited to business data processing. Insurance companies were among the most vigorous lobbyists for such a code; so was the biggest data processor of all, the federal government. The computer industry and the government worked jointly on this project (some of the work was done at the Pentagon); the result was the COmmon Business Oriented Language, or COBOL.

BASICally Speaking

Let's take a look at how a computer is programmed in a language that was designed to make things easier for those with *no* background whatsoever in computers. It also happens to be the language that comes as standard equipment with most personal computers: Beginner's All-purpose Symbolic Instruction Code—or just plain BASIC.

Developed at Dartmouth College in the mid-1960s as a teaching tool, BASIC has become the most popular and well known of all the computer languages. It uses very simple, elementary algebra, and it is concise and altogether unintimidating. Unfortunately, it has not been standardized. The version of BASIC found with any particular brand of personal computer will probably differ slightly from that found with other manufacturers' models. They are like dialects of a spoken language. Fortunately, these different versions are close enough so that programs written for one brand of machine can usually be adapted to run on another with only slight modification. (This applies only to programs you write yourself. Prepackaged, "ready-to-run" software will only work on the brand of computer for which it was written.)

A BASIC Program

So, to begin at the beginning. What if we wanted to enter the preceding sentence into the computer and reproduce it on the terminal screen? We write out our instructions to the computer as statements, telling the machine to do such and such a thing—in this case, print the sentence. We must also number the statements: each BASIC statement is consecutively numbered, usually in increments of ten in order to leave space for inserting other steps later on if it becomes necessary to alter the program. Thus we would type on the terminal keyboard:

10 PRINT "SO, TO BEGIN AT THE BEGINNING."[1]

After we've typed each statement on the keyboard, examined the results on the screen, and are satisfied that it's what we want, we press a key that says either ENTER or RETURN (like a typewriter carriage return key). This tells the computer to put the information into its main memory. We'll assume here that the button says ENTER. We push it and our statement goes into the computer, which is now ready for the next line. Since this program is a one-liner, we have no more statements; we just want the machine to run the program.

So we type out the word RUN and look at the screen to see the results of our program. Nothing happens. In fact, we could sit here until kingdom come and still not see anything happen. That's because we forgot to press ENTER. We must do that after *every* command we give the machine; that's how we instruct it to take in the command and follow through with it. We press ENTER and almost instantly we see on the screen:

SO, TO BEGIN AT THE BEGINNING.

Numbers are handled in somewhat the same way, except that the computer will perform the operations indicated and give us the result of those opera-

[1] Some machines print only capital letters.

tions rather than just reproduce the numbers we type in. Another one-line program will make this clear. We type:

    10 PRINT 2 + 2

We press ENTER. Then we press RUN, and then ENTER again. The screen quickly displays:

    4

Actually, for a one-line calculation you can use the computer as you would a pocket calculator by resorting to something called direct entry. That means you can simply type

    PRINT 2 + 2

without a statement number, enter and run it, and have 4 appear as your answer.

By using simple algebra, we can get the computer to do some useful things for us. This involves setting up variables, which are usually indicated by a single letter, as in

    LET X = 5

This means that a memory location is set aside and called X and its contents is 5. Remember the analogy we used to show how the computer works? This is like taking one of the shoe boxes on the memory table, labeling the box "X," and putting five marbles in it.

More than one variable can be used in a program, as in the following:

110

```
10 LET X = 5

20 LET Y = 3

30 LET A = X − Y

40 PRINT A
```

When we type this into the computer it assigns a
location for the X variable and one for the Y variable,
and sets the contents of those memory locations at
the quantities we have specified, namely 5 and 3.
Then it sets up a memory location for A, evaluates the
expression A = X − Y (it already knows, or "remembers" what X and Y equal), sets the contents of memory location A equal to X − Y (that is, 5 − 3), and,
according to our instructions, prints out the contents
of A:

2

We said that X, Y, and A are variables; that means
they can change. The name of each memory location
will remain the same, but their contents can be altered
(shoe box A will remain shoe box A, but we can take
out the two marbles and replace them with another
quantity).

Let's add a few lines to our program:

```
10 LET X = 5

20 LET Y = 3

30 LET A = X − Y

40 PRINT A

50 LET B = X + Y

60 PRINT B
```

When we run this we get:

2

8

Through line 40 this program is the same as the preceding one. Step 40 retrieved the contents of memory location A and printed it out: 2. Line 50 says that we still have that memory location called A, but now we want to set up a new variable, B, equal to the sum of X and Y instead of their difference. The contents of locations X and Y haven't changed; they're still 5 and 3. Those figures are added by the computer to get the new variable, B: 8. We put two PRINT statements in our program so we get two answers: the value of A at line 40 and the value of B at line 60.

What if we had left out line 60? All we would get as an answer would be 2. The computer anticipates nothing, does nothing unless it is instructed to do so in a program line.

Dealing with Words

There are two different kinds of variables. Numerical variables (like the ones we just used) are represented on most machines by one or two letters. We usually ask the machine to carry out some kind of mathematical operation on them, such as addition. But we might want variables that are not to be operated on mathematically, but rather moved around or sorted in some way. They could be names that we want alphabetized or voter registration records that we want arranged by zip codes. These are called string variables.

In BASIC these are always enclosed in quotation

marks so the computer knows that they are not numbers to be operated on, but rather are a string of characters to be moved around, sorted, or whatever else we want done with them—but kept intact as a string. We would not, for example, want zip codes added together as if they were numerical variables.

Just as numerical variables can be represented by letters such as X or Y, string variables can also be symbolized. In BASIC, this is done by using a letter and a dollar sign, as in C$. This simply says that we have set up a memory location called C$ and its contents will be whatever we specify. We could have used this in our first program:

```
10 LET C$ =. "SO, TO BEGIN AT THE BEGINNING."

20 PRINT C$
```

When we run it we see on the screen:

```
SO, TO BEGIN AT THE BEGINNING.
```

Now we can begin to appreciate the "alphanumeric" quality of the computer. The memory locations in the computer's main memory can hold words as well as numbers. The letters of each word, just like the digits of each number, are represented in the machine by a binary code of 1s and 0s; they are converted into that code automatically when we type them in. But letters and numbers are both moved around inside the computer in the same way. When they leave as output they are converted back into the form that we are familiar with; that's what we see on the terminal screen.

Lest we cultivate a fetish about beginning at the beginning, let's pick out a new string variable and, as the saying goes, "do a number on it." The classical composer Paul Dukas wrote a symphonic poem called "The Sorcerer's Apprentice." Let's program it.

```
10 LET B$ = "THE SORCERER'S APPRENTICE"

20 PRINT B$
```

And when we run it our obedient servant displays:

```
THE SORCERER'S APPRENTICE
```

The story upon which this music is based tells of a sorcerer's apprentice who watches his master command a broom to fetch pails of water to fill his bath. When the sorcerer is away, the apprentice decides to play. He gets the broom to fill his bath, too, except that there's a problem. He can't remember the magic word to make the broom stop. Soon the room is flooded. Fortunately the boss comes home just in time to say the word, turn the broom off, and save his apprentice, who is about to go down for the last time.

(In 1940 Walt Disney released a movie called *Fantasia*, a combination of animation and music conducted by Leopold Stokowski. One sequence in the film featured this tale. The apprentice was played by Mickey Mouse.)

There is a point to the story. To illustrate it, let's add a line to our program:

```
10 LET B$ = "THE SORCERER'S APPRENTICE"

20 PRINT B$

30 GO TO 20
```

Remember, a computer proceeds systematically through a program, step by numbered step, until it reaches the end. But where is the end of this program? The machine sets aside a memory location called B$ and its contents is the string variable "The Sorcerer's Apprentice." That's done by step 10. The next step, line 20, retrieves the contents of that memory location and prints it out. Then it goes to line 30, which tells it to go back to line 20, which again tells it to print out the contents of memory location B$. Then it proceeds to line 30, which tells it to go back to line 20, which again tells it to print out the contents of memory location B$. Then it proceeds to line 30, which tells it to go back to line 20—and on and on. Charles Babbage described this as "the machine chasing its own tail."

We run the program and get:

THE SORCERER'S APPRENTICE

THE SORCERER'S APPRENTICE

THE SORCERER'S APPRENTICE

THE SORCERER'S APPRENTICE

THE SORCERER'S APPRENTICE

ad infinitum.

This is known as an endless loop. It's like the broom that couldn't be stopped. The computer will keep running through the program and printing out that string variable until it collapses, or we hit a key labeled BREAK (or, on some computers, ESCAPE), pull the plug, or take an ax to the machine.

In truth there's a neater way to put the lid on. We can write the equivalent of the sorcerer's magic word into the program. We can specify how many times we want this, or anything else within the program to be repeated. This is how it's done:

```
10 FOR X = 1 TO 10

20 LET B$ = "THE SORCERER'S APPRENTICE"

30 PRINT B$

40 NEXT X

50 END
```

This is called a FOR/NEXT loop. Line 10 will control the duration of the loop. It says that whatever follows is going to be done a total of ten times, starting with this, the first run-through. Lines 20 and 30 are the same as before and will print out the string variable every time we loop through the program. Line 40 says to the computer that the program should be run through again. It's as if we had written GO TO 20. The program will run through again and again until it completes the tenth statement of "The Sorcerer's Apprentice"—at which point the computer executes the command in line 40, NEXT X, and discovers that it has reached the limit we set for it. Then it will stop.

What we have done, in effect, is set up the memory location X as a counting variable. It will count, from 1 to 10, the number of times that the machine will print the string variable. Every time the computer runs through the last line in the program, the contents of memory location X is upped by 1, until it reaches

10. The final result will be ten of "The Sorcerer's Apprentice" instead of an infinite number.

Using a Conditional Branch

We could have accomplished the same thing if we had written a conditional branch into the program. It would look like this:

```
10 LET X = 0

20 LET B$ = "THE SORCERER'S APPRENTICE"

30 LET X = X + 1

40 PRINT B$

50 IF X = 10 THEN STOP

60 GO TO 30
```

Lines 20 and 40 are the same as before and will serve to print the string variable every time the computer runs through the program. Line 10 sets up memory location X and sets the content at 0. Line 30 increases the value of X by 1. Since it started at 0, it would now be equal to 1. (X = X + 1, incidentally, is not algebra; it's an instruction to the computer, not an equation.)

Line 50 sets up the conditional branch. Every time the program is run this line will compare the contents of location X to 10; when they are equal, the program will stop running. In the meantime, line 60 sends the program back to line 30, which increases the value of X by 1.

Some Practical Uses for BASIC

These are some of the elements of BASIC programming. Although it may not be suited to handling very complicated mathematical calculations or the data processing needs of big business, it can certainly be put to use for many applications. Using only the routines we've seen here, we can at least get a taste of BASIC's value as a programming language.

Suppose we wanted to print out automatically a table converting miles to kilometers and we wanted it done for each mile up to one hundred. Using a calculator we would have to perform one hundred separate calculations. Using a computer, we could first check an almanac to see how many kilometers there are in one mile. That's the only formula we need. The program takes advantage of the FOR/NEXT loop and is all of three lines:

```
10 FOR X = 1 TO 100

20 PRINT X; "MILES ="; X*1.609; "KILOMETERS"

30 NEXT X
```

This time line 10 does two things for us. It's a counting variable; it will control the number of times the program is run and stop it at 100. It is also the mileage figure. It will be used in line 20 to increase the number of miles being converted by 1, each time the program is repeated. Line 20 may look a little complicated but it really isn't. It's just carefully punctuated so that the output message gives us the kilometer equivalent in an easily readable form.

The "MILES=" is in quotes so the computer will simply print it as is each time. The asterisk in X*1.609 is computerese for multiply (the "×" sign could be confused with the letter "X"). This expression will be evaluated each time the program is repeated with a value of X that has been increased by 1 and is equal to the miles figure. If this were the 49th time, X would equal 49; when 49 is multiplied by 1.609 we learn how many kilometers there are in 49 miles. Finally, "KILOMETERS" is in quotes so that it too, just like "MILES=", will be reproduced exactly as we have written it, with each new calculation.

We run the program and get:

1 MILES = 1.609 KILOMETERS

2 MILES = 3.218 KILOMETERS

3 MILES = 4.827 KILOMETERS

—and it will keep on going for another 97 miles until we reach 100. If we had wanted this calculated for every half mile up to 100, we would have inserted STEP .5 at the end of line 10 and the computer would have increased X by .5 instead of 1 each time the program was run.

Did the bad grammar ("1 MILES") in the first line of the output bother you? It might make a difference to a business with a computer terminal for answering customer's questions on a variety of subjects. One could imagine, for example, a bank with that kind of set-up to show its depositors how their money would grow over the years in certain kinds of accounts. That program would not be too different from the one that converts miles to kilometers. One variable would increase with each run of the program, for units of time such as years, half years, etc. Another variable would at first be equal to the amount deposited; a formula in the program would add interest to that amount and every time the program was run the amount on deposit would be the old figure plus the interest.

If we want to improve the computer's grammar (actually our own, since we wrote the program), we can modify the program by adding two lines at the beginning, which is a good example of why the lines are numbered in increments of 10 rather than 1:

```
3 LET X = 1

5 PRINT X; "MILE="; X*1.609; "KILOMETERS"

10 FOR X = 2 TO 100

20 PRINT X; "MILES="; X*1.609; "KILOMETERS"

30 NEXT X
```

When run, the program produces:

```
1 MILE = 1.609 KILOMETERS

2 MILES = 3.218 KILOMETERS

3 MILES = 4.827 KILOMETERS
```

and so on.

We simply dealt with that first mile separately. The computer prints that one out first and then goes into the loop that will end at 100. Since the first mile is taken care of, we start the loop at number 2. The computer, incidentally, works so fast that there will be no visible pause after the first two steps are run. To anyone looking at the terminal screen the table will print out smoothly from the beginning. Only we the programmers know what changes were made behind the scenes.

What if we wanted to know the equivalent number of kilometers for any given mileage figure without printing out a whole table? And similarly, what if bank patrons wanted to know the value of their savings at a given rate of interest after a specific length of time without going through all other time intervals in between?

For this we use the INPUT command. We program the computer so that it will ask us for the information it needs to make the computation. A program to accomplish this could read:

```
10 PRINT "TO CONVERT MILES TO KILOMETERS, ENTER THE
DISTANCE IN MILES"

20 INPUT X

30 PRINT "THE DISTANCE IS"; X; "MILES"

40 PRINT "THAT EQUALS"; X*1.609 "KILOMETERS"
```

When the program is run, first we see this:

```
TO CONVERT MILES TO KILOMETERS, ENTER THE DISTANCE IN
MILES
```

At some place on the screen we will also see a question mark or some other symbol (this depends on the computer model) which indicates that we must supply some information. In effect, the computer is asking us to give the value of X. Let's say that we are going to Europe and we want to do some backpacking. The most we've ever covered in two days in the United States is 27 miles. But European maps are marked in kilometers. How far can we go? We type 27; the computer then continues to run the program. The final result on the screen is:

TO CONVERT MILES TO KILOMETERS, ENTER THE DISTANCE IN MILES

THE DISTANCE IS 27 MILES

THAT EQUALS 44.443 KILOMETERS

The bank program would of course be worded differently and it would ask you for several pieces of information: the amount of your initial investment, the current interest rate of the account you are choosing, and the maturity date of the certificate. Then a formula built into that program would calculate the value of your account at that projected maturity date.

Even in a short program, it is easy to make a mistake. We might forget the second of a set of parentheses, or leave out a comma, or try to use a certain command in a situation in which the computer can't utilize that command. In a program of several hundred lines there is an even greater likelihood that that will happen. The computer is completely unforgiving of such errors. A misplaced punctuation mark means your answers will not appear in the form you had thought you were specifying. A misused command will actually elicit a rebuke from the machine. In some computers a message will appear on the screen stating that you had used an "illegal statement." Talk about guilt! Other computers may merely charge you with a "syntax error."

Sometimes a program may contain a "logical error" that isn't recognized by the computer as an error per se and only shows up when the program is run. Our problem with "1 MILES" was a mild version of that.

All these things are "bugs" to the computer programmer. Going through a newly written program and taking out the bugs is called debugging. The term goes back to the beginning of the computer era, when on a summer's evening in 1945 Dr. Grace Murray Hopper was working on the Mark I at Harvard. The machine wasn't functioning properly. "Finally," she recalls, "someone located the trouble spot and, using ordinary tweezers, removed the problem—a two-inch moth. From then on, when anything went wrong with a computer, we said it had bugs in it." She's been challenged on this, but she refers all skeptics to her Navy logbook where the offending—but now historic—insect is neatly taped to the appropriate page.

Beyond BASIC

Although BASIC has become quite popular due to the dramatic increase in personal computer use, the main programming languages for science and industry are still FORTRAN and COBOL. We can understand why there should be a variety of languages rather than one universal one if we think of how we might prepare to take courses in different subjects. For math we might get graph paper, a booklet with trigonometric tables, a pocket calculator with special keys for math functions, and perhaps a compass. For a course in accounting we might need accountant's note paper, a ledger, a dictionary of business terms, and a calculator with functions related to business problems.

Each computer language is designed to fill the needs of people working in a specific field. Different subject areas make different demands on a language for handling variables, large amounts of data, and the formatting of output in a manner that is understandable to and usable by someone working in that field. The compilers that translate instructions from a particular high-level language into machine language are programs themselves and can be designed for peak efficiency when their use is limited to relevant problems.

BASIC seems to have been modeled more on FORTRAN than on any other language. In appearance, a FORTRAN program resembles a BASIC program. However, FORTRAN requires that the programmer devote a good deal of time to specifying how the output is to be formatted; the output devices themselves also must be named in the program. FORTRAN also has a powerful and succinct technique for dealing with loops called a DO statement, which differs little from a FOR/NEXT loop.

FORTRAN is not good at handling string variables, the main stock in trade of business and government. Magazine subscription information, personnel records, customer files—indeed, almost everything you can find in a file drawer is usually more in need of sorting, classifying, arranging, and retrieval than it is of arithmetic operations. COBOL was created to handle these processes.

COBOL's commands are designed with large files of information in mind. Programs written in COBOL are structured to resemble sentences and paragraphs. Programs are divided into four divisions:

1. *Identification:* who wrote the program, when and where it was done, etc.

2. *Environment:* describing in detail all input and output devices to be used.

3. *Data:* describing memory locations to be used; goes into detail and specifies input and output formats.

4. *Procedures:* enumerating the operations to be carried out and describing the logic behind them.

The language used in COBOL programs tends to be close to business English. The programs are long—three to four times the length of a typical BASIC program—and very wordy. A program written in COBOL is far from elegant. In fact, if truth will out, they are terribly dreary to look at. But when it comes to names, addresses, and similar data—the fuel of our information-based economy—it is an efficient language and it gets the job done. Its value has been proven in practice: it is the most widely used of all business programming languages.

Over the years attempts have been made to supplant FORTRAN and COBOL. IBM's PL/1 (Programming Language 1) was an effort at producing a universal language. APL (A Programming Language), also from IBM, is math-oriented. RPG (Report Program Generator) is easy to learn and has been used extensively in dealing with large files about which reports are required. ALGOrithmic Language (or ALGOL), another mathematics language, is used extensively in Europe. Pascal, a complex, highly structured general-purpose language named for the mathematician, has come on strong in recent years to challenge BASIC in the personal computer field. And still they come, delighting the computer dictionary makers. Would you believe LISP, MAD, SNOBOL, SYNFUL, and LAFF?

The User-Friendliest Language

The ultimate goal of the computer industry—a goal that will not be attained for many years—is the user-friendliest language of all: the translator program that can convert plain, unadorned English into machine language. "Look at all the people in the world who know English," Larry Harris of the Artificial Intelligence Corporation has remarked, "and then count all the people who know FORTRAN and BASIC." His company, coincidentally, has developed a program called Intellect that stores rules of grammar as well as a limited vocabulary. It analyzes input inquiries made in English and converts them into subprograms for accessing information. But the system keeps tripping over pronouns and takes requests for information too literally. For example, if a company president asked the computer in Intellect, "Can you tell me the names of our ten best clients?" the computer would respond, "Yes." Pause; end of message.

Digital smart alecks are not appreciated in the business world and sales of this program have been sluggish.

Programming: Art or Science?

Computer programming is only thirty years old; as a discipline it is still in its infancy. Only in the last decade have programmers begun to address the question of whether or not to standardize program-writing methods.

Given the same problem to be analyzed and coded for the computer, two sets of systems analysts and programmers will not necessarily come up with identical programs. There's usually more than one way to handle data and more than one logical design. Programming is both an art and a craft, say many observers. "Computer programs are not bound by natural laws in their manipulation of data," contends Joel Birnbaum, director of computer research at Hewlett Packard. "The programmer may cause practically any arbitrary sequence of logical and arithmetic manipulation to be performed on the data, as long as the results remain within the range of values acceptable to the hardware."

Structured Programming

This is not the prevailing view among software producers. Since the late 1960s most programmers have consciously sought to avoid the idiosyncratic in order to write programs that can be understood by anybody, even twenty years after the program is written and the programmer is not around to explain the reasoning behind any given step or section. Structured (or top-down) programming, as this concept is called, involves the use of a main (or stem) program listing the general steps used to solve the problem, with details divided up into sections (or modules) that are "plugged" into the main program at the appropriate point. The emphasis is on making clear the relationship of each part of the program to all other parts. Pascal, a language often used with personal computers, was designed to take advantage of this approach.

IBM's Glenn Bacon recently compared the two styles of programming, likening early programming to "a bowl of spaghetti as contrasted to a set of building blocks with well-defined interfaces."

Art or science, programming has posed a fascinating problem for the law. With the increasing prominence of software has come an intense examination of its basic nature. If a computer without a program is like a brain without a thought, is the program an inherent part of the machine? Without the program, is a computer anything at all?

Copyrighting Programs

This question is more than academic. The computer copyright act of 1980 defines a program as a "set of statements or instructions to be used directly or indirectly in a computer in order to bring about a certain result." The specific steps in any program can be copyrighted; but should an especially ingenious logical design for solving a problem—the general step-by-step logical solution for solving all problems of that type—be eligible for a patent? In other words, is a program an invention? Can a rival company change a few numbers but keep the general scheme which had been so carefully and expensively worked out by another company—without paying royalties? In the video game business, for example, should a popular game like Pac-Man have to contend with virtual copies with names like "Munch-Man," "Chomp-Man," and "Bite-

Man"—games run on programs only slightly different from the original one that runs the little yellow gobbler? In fact, Atari, which markets Pac-Man, has gone to court over the situation and won.

The courts have resisted the patenting of program designs. Ernest Keet, the president of National CSS, one of the 4,000 computer service companies that, combined, do about $15 billion of business annually, much of it involving programming for other companies, has written: "This is the first time in history that people are seeking the mass sale of intellectual property in other than printed form. . . . You don't have to copy line for line to steal design concept. Copyright only protects your particular expression of the idea, not the idea itself."

Aside from the question of whether or not programs can be patented, defining them as tangible pieces of capital would also make companies that produce them eligible for certain tax credits. Many in the industry agree with Martin Goetz of Applied Data Research: "Software is a machine component of a computer system, similar to a computer circuit component or a terminal component, or a disk component." He and his colleagues say, in effect, that if it looks like a duck, walks like a duck, and quacks like a duck, certain logical conclusions should be drawn. But so far, although the U.S. Patent Office has begun to relent, the courts have said that the essence of a program is in the ethereal realm of ideal forms; to them it looks like a swan.

CHAPTER 7

TELECOMMUNICA- TIONS—IT'S JUST A PHONE CALL AWAY

In 1940, an early binary computer developed by George Stibitz at Bell Labs was demonstrated at Dartmouth College in Hanover, New Hampshire—via telegraph from New York City. This demonstration was the first experiment in operating a computer by means of telecommunications—that is, communicating electronically from a distance.

Since then, the development of networks of wire, cable, glass fiber, microwave transmitters, and satellites has been as critical to computer use as advances in computer hardware itself have been. What highways were to the automobile, telecommunications networks have become for the computer. Each new distance-shortening method has substantially increased the power of these technologies and has broadened their impact on society as well. Of the interconnection of distant computers and their linkage to other electronic devices, journalist John Wicklein has written that: "All modes of communication we humans have devised since the beginnings of our humanity are coming together now into a single electronic system, driven by computers."

The Wired Society

Increasing dependence on the linkage between computers is turning ours into a "wired society." According to one computer expert, we may already have gone beyond the point where our economy could function without this interconnection; our very physical safety has even been entrusted to a vast digital communications network, the one that makes up our nuclear missile early warning and response system.

But the impact of this electronic interconnection is perhaps felt most intensely in an area which is less life-threatening, but certainly as critical to the orderly functioning of the world—that of information storage and retrieval. And as a result, the computer's data storage and transmission function is rapidly becoming as important as its original computing function.

Due to increased computational speed, time sharing, and new input technologies, data can now be stored most efficiently and retrieved with tremendous facility. Because electronic storage is quicker, neater, and defies distance barriers, record-keeping and fact-gathering tasks are increasingly being turned over to computers. As a result, businesses and individuals alike now depend on timely information provided by "electronic libraries" and various public access databases.

The ease with which today's larger computers can be accessed by several individuals simultaneously—many or all of whom are nowhere near the machine itself—is the result of two technological innovations. The first is computers capable of handling more than one program or query at a time; the second is new levels of sophistication in a communications network that has been in use for some time: the telephone system.

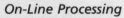

Time Sharing

Today most computer users are "on line"; this means they are interacting with the computer by means of a direct line to the central processing unit, usually through a terminal keyboard. Response from the central system is displayed directly on the terminal's video screen, all of this occurring with at most a few seconds' delay.

On-Line Processing

If a program is being run, the software is inserted on a nearby disk drive, the relevant information is input on the keyboard and the results appear almost immediately on the screen.

If information is being retrieved from a database, the request is typed in and the response appears on the screen almost immediately.

But in the early years of computer use, this method had not yet been developed. Data that was to be sorted, stored, or arithmetically computed had to be

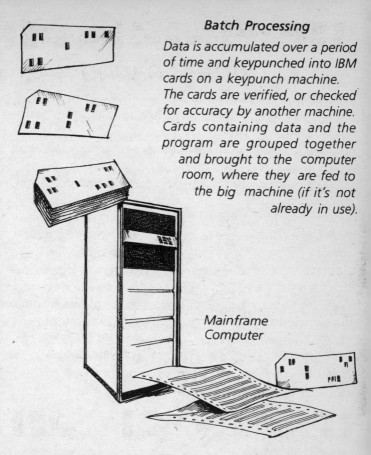

Batch Processing

Data is accumulated over a period of time and keypunched into IBM cards on a keypunch machine. The cards are verified, or checked for accuracy by another machine. Cards containing data and the program are grouped together and brought to the computer room, where they are fed to the big machine (if it's not already in use).

Mainframe Computer

The output will be in the form of a printout and/or more cards.

accumulated in large batches over a period of time and recorded on IBM cards, which were brought to the computer itself. There was frequently a waiting period for processing because other work had priority. Batch processing, as this operation is called, was time consuming, and the results of a project were often not available for hours or even days. Many of today's computer applications were out of the question then. (Although electric utility companies, for example, still generate monthly bills by batch processing methods because time is not crucial, they can call up instantly a customer's usage and payment record, an impossibility if batch processing were the only available option.)

By the mid-1960s computers with larger memory units could handle more than one program at a time. Through time sharing, which is made possible by partitioning a larger main memory so it can hold both programs and data from many different users simultaneously, a computer's resources could now be used by several different operators at the same time. The central processing unit executes instructions from one program for a brief time before going to the next and then the next in round-robin fashion, until finally, having devoted part of each second to each different program, all have been run to completion. Because the computer works so quickly, users have the impression that the machine has been working on their project alone.

Distributed Processing

The development of the disk as a mass (or secondary) storage device enabled rapid data retrieval without running through a length of magnetic tape. (Despite the use of disks for quick access to data, tape continued to be used for long-term off-line storage.) The use of the terminal keyboard to enter data also meant that records could be updated continuously without the

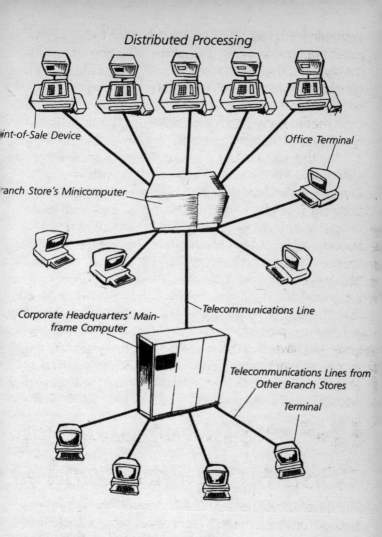

Distributed Processing

Point-of-Sale Device

Office Terminal

Branch Store's Minicomputer

Corporate Headquarters' Mainframe Computer

Telecommunications Line

Telecommunications Lines from Other Branch Stores

Terminal

delays and labor inherent in batch processing. Data processing, no longer confined by batch processing methods to the company computer room, could now be performed wherever convenient—wherever a terminal could be linked by telecommunications lines to a large central processing unit. This is known as "distributed processing."

With the arrival of minicomputers in the mid-1960s distributed processing really came into its own. Computers were rapidly becoming as valuable for information storage as they were for number crunching, since the lower-level processing needs of many businesses did not call for the powerful central processing unit and huge memory facilities of a mainframe. Now individual departments could each have their own independent systems, with additional communications hook-ups to a central company unit for accessing corporation-wide files or performing calculations beyond the minicomputer's capabilities.

During the past two decades some computer systems have turned into vast complexes of interconnected units doing different things for different people. A good example is the branch store of a large retail chain, where point-of-sale devices record charge purchases and instantly send this information to the store's minicomputer, which is located in the store office. Employees there use individual terminals connected to that minicomputer to process daily sales and inventory figures. Information from all stores in the chain is transmitted to the corporate headquarters, where company executives use a mainframe computer to make sales projections and analyze the overall inventory situation. If diagrammed, the computer communications network used by a large company might look like a vast and intricate spider web.

Handshakes and Protocol

To understand how a secretary in St. Louis can type into a terminal a request for sales figures from the main corporate computer in San Diego, we must examine the means by which computers are connected to communications networks, the method of data transmission over those networks, and the nature of the networks themselves.

A company or institution large enough to make substantial use of data communications lines will usually need a separate computer just to act as a communications control unit. This machine is the interface between the terminals and computers at one location, and the rest of the world. This "front-end processor," as it is often called, must be all things to all computers. If the machines at the receiving end are of a different make and operate on a different system from the computers at the sending end, then the front-end processor must make the proper connections. Nineteen subcommittees of the American National Standards Institute are currently wrestling with these "language barriers"; in the meantime, however, computers must signal each other to agree on how to send and receive information. As in diplomacy between nations, the smoothing out of differences is eased by the establishment of mutually acceptable standards of behavior—in this case a sort of electronic courtesy code called a "protocol"—exchanged by the

Data Transmission

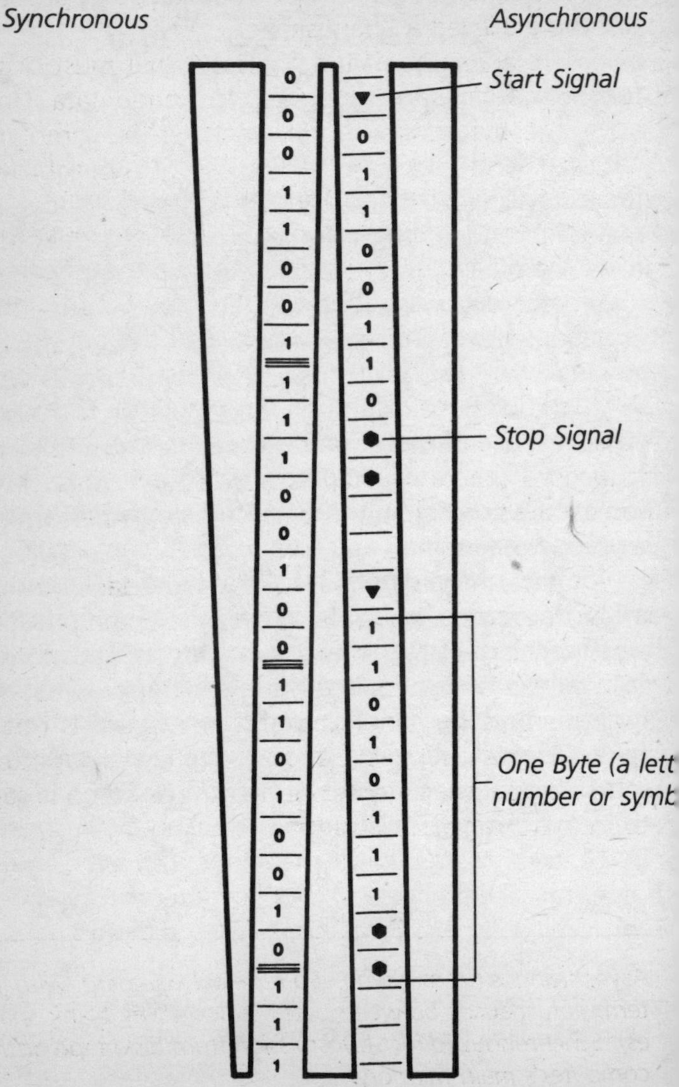

Synchronous

Asynchronous

Start Signal

Stop Signal

One Byte (a lett
number or symb

computers at either end of the communications line. When the machines have exchanged check signals and are transmitting in the same manner, they are said to have achieved a "handshake."

Here are some of the processes that must occur for the machines to link up and exchange data. Until now, the bytes of information have been moving within the computer with all of the bits in each byte traveling together in parallel. The bits must now be rearranged—lined up one after another in serial order to be transmitted over a single wire.

If transmission speed is to be slow and irregular, as it would be if a message were being typed out on a terminal, bits would be sent at irregular intervals with extra bits at the beginning and end of each byte to indicate that one whole character were about to be or had just been transmitted. This is called "asynchronous transmission" (as in "out of synch")—performed at irregular intervals.

If data from main memory or secondary storage at one location is being sent directly to a computer at another location, the information can be transmitted faster and with a steadier flow, since the idiosyncratic movement of human fingers at a keyboard is not a factor. In this case, bits are forwarded at regular intervals in byte-long bunches and the transmission is said to be synchronous.

Asynchronous (from typing at a terminal keyboard, with intermittent pauses between bytes indicated by blank spaces). Synchronous (direct transmission from disk, tape or the computer's main memory).

Transmission Networks: New Uses For the Telephone

Telephone system lines carry much of today's telecommunications load. The network of connections that makes up that system, however, was originally built to handle the human voice by means of an analog signal; the needs of today's computers, which in a sense are simpler, were not anticipated then.

Voice and Data Transmission Over Telephone

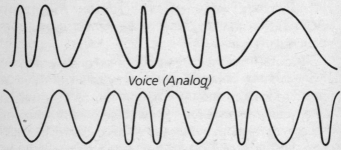

Voice (Analog)

Data (Digital)

The wider waves are 0s—there are fewer of them per second because they are represented by a lower frequency.

When you speak into the mouthpiece of a telephone, your voice is converted into a modulated (continuously altered) current that is demodulated when it reaches the person you are calling so they can hear it once again as speech. Binary digits, of course, are digital signals, which in order to fit into the telephone's mode of transmission must be converted to an analog signal. They have no regional accent, stutter, or peculiar breathing pattern; they are just discrete bits of information that, like a voice on the telephone, must be moved from one end of the line to the other.

The communications device that converts the digital signal at the sending end into an analog signal for transmission, and then from analog back to digital at the receiving end is called a modem, short for modulator-demodulator. Digital traffic is simpler to transmit, since the modem has only two kinds of information to send out: 1s and 0s. In most cases, each bit is converted into one of two audible tones; the "1" tone is usually a higher frequency than the "0" tone. The modem could, for example, be signaling "do" for every "0" and "re" or "mi" for every "1."

The telephone system—dubbed recently by *Science* magazine "the largest and most complex mechanism on the earth"—offers a possible 6,000,000,000,000,000 connections and over the years has cost about $170 billion to put in place. Since the 1890s, telephone connections have been made by a series of electromechanical relays that progressively narrow down the number of circuits to whom callers can be connected as they dial each successive digit of a phone number. When the last digit is dialed, there is only one circuit left—the one leading to the phone the caller is trying to ring up.

Direct long-distance dialing dates from 1951 (coincidentally, the year of UNIVAC's debut), and since 1973 more than half of all long-distance traffic in the telephone system has consisted of computer-to-computer communication. In recent years the electromechanical relays themselves have begun to be replaced by heavy-duty computers that connect up the circuits in a direct, electronic fashion without the need for relays (with their moving parts). The history of telephone technology has paralleled that of the computer, and the vast telephone network has actually become the biggest computer system in the world.

The telephone system is not without its shortcomings when used to connect a computer in one place with a processor in another. For one thing, noise and static on the lines can threaten message integrity. This can be countered by adding a "parity" or check bit to each byte, thus enabling the receiving computer to determine that the bytes it receives are the same as the ones that were sent.

Another shortcoming is slow transmission speed over telephone wires. The rate of data transmission is expressed in bits per second, or bps (sometimes written as so many "baud," a unit of telegraph measurement which is virtually the same as bps), the maximum rate dependent on the band width (or information-handling capacity) of the transmitting medium. In practice, this means a maximum rate of 4,800 bps over regular telephone lines; usually it is performed at a slower rate to decrease the effect of possible electromagnetic interference (300 baud is not uncommon).

An alternative to the ordinary switched (or dialed) lines accessible to every telephone user are special leased transmission lines. These are useful for big companies with a high volume of data to be communicated between branch offices and plants. Static is easier to control on these private direct-connection lines. Transmission rates are also higher—a possible maximum of 9,600 bps.

Microwaves and Light Beams

Other more advanced technologies offer even speedier transmission. Over short distances—within an office building, for example—coaxial cable can carry 1.5 million bps. Microwave transmission may be used over longer distances and attain even greater speed, although regular telephone lines may be required at both the sending and receiving ends to link the computers with the microwave transmitters. (The saucer-shaped antennas seen occasionally on top of tall buildings or towers are used for microwave transmitting and receiving.)

More and more communication satellites are coming into the picture, and in the past decade they have become an increasingly vital link in communications between computers. American Telephone and Telegraph (AT&T) extended its reach into outer space some time ago; the Satellite Business System, a joint venture of IBM, the Communications Satellite Corporation (COMSAT), and the Aetna Life and Casualty Company began putting their satellites up in the early 1980s. Satellites which relay microwaves have a distinct advantage over ground transmitters, which cannot send data past the horizon without a relay station to pass along the signal—a sort of electronic pony express. Satellites transmit signals efficiently over enormous distances and are no slouches when it comes to speed—the digitized contents of the entire Bible can be passed along quicker than you can say "In God We Trust."

Fiber optic transmission, one of the newer technologies to come into play and one which figures to be increasingly important in the future, harkens back to the wire-cable approach. In this case, though, it's light rather than an electric current that carries the signal. Harry Gray, head of United Technologies Corporation, has said that "theoretically, one light beam could carry all phone calls and radio and TV programs in North America simultaneously."

Fiber optic transmission is based on the principle that the frequency of light can be modulated to carry information just as an electrical signal can be altered continuously to convey a message. High-frequency beams are sent through narrow glass fiber cables, whose inside surfaces help pass the light along by reflecting it. Up to 200 million bits per second can be transmitted through these cables, which also happen to be immune to electromagnetic disruption. The technology has already been perfected to the point where an undersea optical transmission cable to Europe may be a reality in the near future.

The urgent need for transmission technology specifically adapted to digital signals becomes clearer as we move further into the era of distributed processing. The establishment of communications networks whose structures allow maximally efficient digital transmission has proceeded apace over the past decade. Like leased telephone lines, these new networks suppress electromagnetic interference and permit greater transmission speeds than regular telephone lines. They offer a cheap method of data transmission for high-volume users, and unlike private leased lines, these public networks can offer access to any other computer tied to the network—simply by means of dialing. Timeshare's Timenet and GTE's Telenet have dominated this field, although AT&T has been putting together its own version, the Advanced Information Systems Net 1.

These high-speed digital transmission networks employ a technique called packet switching. This gives users constant access to long-distance lines that are specially modified for sending digital information, without all the cost of private lines. It's like using parcel post to send packages, which come to a post office from many different sources: they're sorted by destination and everything needed for the same city is flown or trucked together until it is dispersed for individual delivery.

The packet-switching network is usually accessed by a local telephone call to the nearest switching station, or "node." There a computer bundles the bytes of information in a message into groups or "packets" (128 bytes is a typical size) that are coded by destination and then passed along through various routes in the system until they reach the switching station in the recipient's area. At that point the data is reassembled into the original message and delivered by local telephone lines. All of this usually takes about one-tenth of a second. The computers on the packet-switching networks help to resolve protocol problems between computers and in effect guide and direct the digital signals safely to their destination.

There are also specialized digital networks dedicated to serving only the needs of a particular industry or group. As with many other advances in computer technology, the Defense Department has led the way. In the 1950s, it set up the Advanced Research Projects Agency Network (ARPANET) to facilitate digital communications between leading universities engaged in defense work. Numerous other private networks have followed. The computers of the world's leading airlines, for example, are linked by SITA, while SWIFT ties together the processors of major banks throughout Europe and the United States to facilitate electronic funds transfers.

Databases and Data Banks

In a society whose economy is increasingly dependent on quick access to information, having a wide-ranging collection of facts and statistics only seconds away can mean everything to the successful functioning of a business. Such access is also vital to research in all fields. Often information is available in only one place, nowhere near the place it is needed. A special kind of computer application using telecommunications lines has been developed to deal with this—the on-line database or data bank.

Database, one of the prime buzz words of the 1980s, refers to the systematic storage of computer-accessible information. The functioning and management of such a storage system can be quite intricate, yet in effect it is nothing more than an electronic version of the familiar office filing system with its cabinets and folders.

Think of all the kinds of records an organization might want to retain: names, addresses, and telephone numbers, as well as other information about its employees, members, or customers. The records would include sales figures broken down into various categories, updated inventory counts, performance records for sales personnel, accounts payable and receivable—the list could go on and on. In a paper filing system each of these groups of figures might be kept in a different room; indeed, a large company might store them in separate buildings or even in different cities. Consulting these records would involve either actually going to where they were kept or calling someone to check them at the other end. The proper filing cabinet, drawer, and folder would have to be located and the information physically retrieved.

The computer, obviously, has made this task considerably easier. Collectively, all the available information forms the database; each group of related data covering one subject area is a file, as in the traditional office terminology. (An example of a typical file might be employee records.) Each group of related data within a file is called a record and is equivalent to the contents of a manila folder in a paper filing system. The name of each record is what would ordinarily be written on that folder, so in the employee file the record would be identified by the name of the employee. Each item of information within a record is a field. An employee's street address and zip code would each be a field; other fields might include the division of the company where the employee works, job classification, salary, etc.

Retrieving information from the database can be accomplished in one of two ways. The first necessi-

Use of a Menu To Access a Data Base

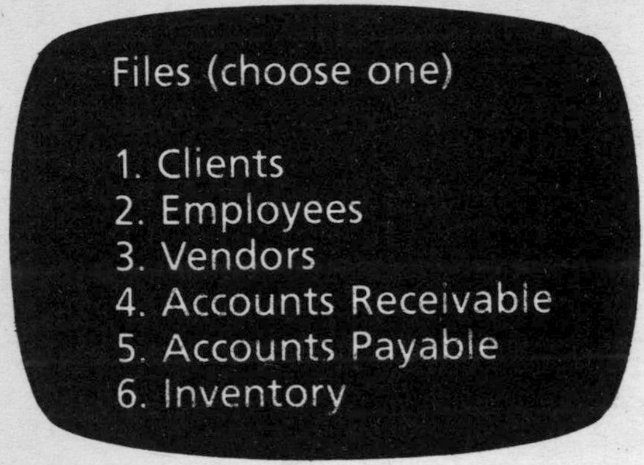

Files (choose one)
1. Clients
2. Employees
3. Vendors
4. Accounts Receivable
5. Accounts Payable
6. Inventory

1

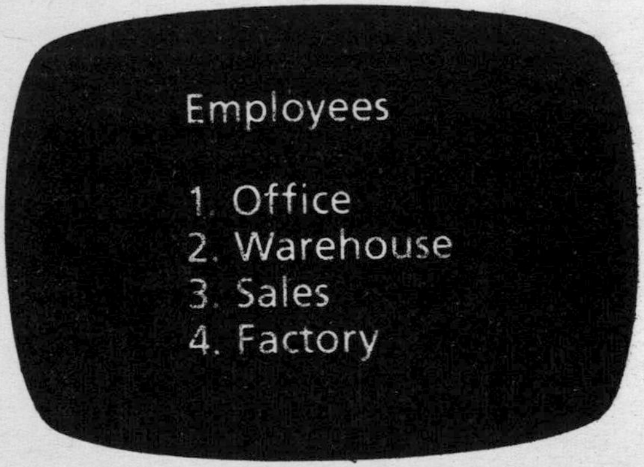

Employees
1. Office
2. Warehouse
3. Sales
4. Factory

2

Factory Employees

1. Production Line
2. Machinist
3. Sheet Metal
4. Maintenance

3

Sheet Metal Division

1. Albert, Sam
2. Andrews, John
3. Astor, Robert
4. Bolingbroke, Thomas

4

```
Employee Record: Andrews, John

Street Address:  100 Elm Street
                 Cliffside Park,
                 New Jersey
Zip:             07010
Title:           Foreman
Wage:            $15/hour
Started:         3/4/79
```

5

tates going down through the hierarchy of information. For example, if you wanted to know John Doe's street address, first you would ask the computer for a list of all the files in the database (this is called a menu). From this you would choose "Employee Records" and then possibly the division in which John Doe works. An alphabetical listing of employees would appear on the screen from which you would select John Doe and then obtain his street address.

This system might be sufficient if there were not too many levels or items to choose from. But a more direct access system would probably be used to locate the address of an employee in a large company. In the relational system, you would type in the employee's name and then link it to the address field in order to get the relevant information onto the screen without further ado. In the same way you could even get the computer to give you a list of all employees who lived on the same street—using the street field as your key—if, for example, you were trying to organize a car pool. The computer's ability to go directly to any field in the information hierarchy, scan it, and deliver the requested data on the screen or in printed copy makes it an extraordinarily powerful tool for business, politics, or virtually any other field of human endeavor.

Electronic Libraries

The vast amounts of information used by both individuals and groups is the stuff libraries are made of. But a library doesn't always have what people want when they want it. It may not be large or specialized enough; the material may be in use or lent out. Interlibrary loan can be used to get locally unavailable books, but it often takes time.

The on-line database retrieval system, on the other hand, is a treasure trove of information, all in one place, that can be accessed from any other place through telecommunications lines. Subscribers to these public-access database services are usually charged by the amount of time spent on line. The system can usually be reached by dialing and then entering a code number and password that control access and identify the user for billing purposes. Elapsed time is usually indicated somewhere on the terminal screen.

On-line databases, which currently number about 1,500, cover the whole panoply of human interests. Lockheed's Dialog is, as Andrew Pollack of the *New*

York Times has put it, an "on-line supermarket" offering access to information on 150 areas of knowledge. Over 2,500 libraries throughout the United States use OCLC (On-line Computer Library Center) to find out what's available and where, when they need to search out a book. Major-league baseball teams can evaluate player performance in any one of twenty-three categories by dialing the Major League Scouting Bureau computer in Minneapolis. Companies that do a lot of shipping by truck have a number of systems available to supply updated shipping rates from all carriers. Several medical libraries are also on line. LEXIS and WESTLAW provide lawyers with information from state and federal case law. There are also other services of more general interest that can be accessed from the home using a personal computer and a regular telephone.

If you think there might be a database that could be useful in your job, or are just curious about what's available, one of these two reference books can probably help you: *Directory of Online Databases* and the *Encyclopedia of Information Systems and Services.*

Some of the most useful sources of information for many kinds of general research are the clipping files of major newspapers and magazines. Business people, government officials, scholars, and students make continued use of the information contained in them. But numerous indexes must be consulted to locate this material, and the microfilmed or bound copies of any of these publications may not be available at a convenient library. However, an on-line database offering instant access to many of these publications, from one computer terminal, has existed for the past decade—the New York Times Information Bank.

In 1973 the data bank signed up its first commercial subscriber. The system, put together by IBM in consultation with the *Times*, contains abstracts of *Times* material going back to 1969, and also makes available abstracted articles for some sixty other publications for almost as long a time span, including the major news and business magazines and newspapers such as the *Washington Post*, the *Wall Street Journal,* and the *Los Angeles Times*.

The system is expensive to use and is probably unavailable in your local library, although some offer it to the public and pass on the cost (currently about $2.30 per minute) to users. Among the several thousand current subscribers are the major broadcasting networks, the Library of Congress, various government agencies and congressional offices, most of the major oil companies, IBM, and the Chase Manhattan Bank.

Subscriber queries usually come in via one of the packet-switching networks, although they can be made by the regular telephone system. All of the data is stored on disks in a room in Parsippany, New Jersey, and although the amount of information stored there—now well over 2 million abstracts—has grown enormously, the space it occupies is virtually the same as a much smaller amount of data took up when the system was initiated.

No special language is needed to retrieve information; queries are made in English. However, the system is based on the use of a special thesaurus of key words that, when typed into the terminal, will call up the desired information. For example, keying in the word "gold" displays the abstracts of articles concerning fluctuations in its price, mining output, and its use as a backing for currency. Any article whose major subject is some use of gold can be accessed merely by entering the word gold or linking it to another major category if that seemed relevant—"archaeology" and gold, for example—to find information about a major discovery of ancient gold relics. In order to reduce the potentially overwhelming number of abstracts that can be retrieved on such a topic, the search can be limited by specifying a range of years or only certain publications.

This mode of access has its limitations. If, for example, you want to know what presidential candidate Ronald Reagan had said about supply-side economics in 1980, you will have a difficult time because that term was not in the thesaurus then. You might get at it by linking Reagan to some economic term, but you would probably be left with more abstracts than it would be worth your while to examine.

In recent years, the *Times* system has been made more user-friendly. A search method called "free text" is now available that enables the researcher—without reference to the thesaurus—to type in any term, alone or linked to another term, and get back to every significant use of the term or terms. And since 1981, complete *New York Times* articles (rather than abstracts) have been available beginning with June 1980 stories, through a separate database.

In some places, there's still room for the old-fashioned filing cabinet. When the Information Bank was being set up, there were those at the *Times* who wanted to get rid of the paper's morgue, but as one company official told me, the news department "did not take kindly" to that plan, and the yellowed clippings are still there.

CHAPTER 8

PERSONAL
COMPUTERS

Not too long ago, the idea of an IBM computer in your living room would probably have seemed bizarre. True, the increasingly smaller and cheaper integrated circuits that had been produced in the 1960s had received wide publicity, as did the development of the microprocessor. But even Alvin Toffler, in his 1970 pop sociology best-seller *Future Shock,* did not predict that these would bear fruit in the form of a "personal" computer.

A 64K RAM chip on a paper clip. The powerful, compact, and relatively inexpensive personal computers now appearing on the market have been made possible by this kind of miniaturization.

By 1974, computer hobbyists were already assembling their own machines. In 1975, the first prewired models were on the market: the Altair 8800 from MITS Corp. and IMSAI's model 8800 (the number refers to the microprocessor used). Both could be programmed in machine language only and were operated by switches rather than keyboards. They were hardly mass market consumer items.

The machine that we are familiar with—the personal computer that instructs, informs, and entertains—dates from 1977, when Steven Wozniak and Steve Jobs, two brash men in their early twenties, introduced the Apple computer. This was a user-friendly microcomputer that was soon firmly established in a growing business and consumer market. The Apple and its early competition, the Commodore PET (Personal Electronic Transactor) and the Radio Shack TRS-80, are still riding the crest of this wave.

Initially, microcomputers were sold primarily to small and medium-sized businesses, but in the last year or two they have penetrated the home market in large numbers. There has even been a swelling chorus of warnings from personal computer manufacturers that families ought to purchase computers to assure their children's computer literacy and hence their place in the world of tomorrow. According to a recent Atari advertisement, for example, "Almost every guidance counselor will tell you that the ability to use and understand computers could be crucial to a child's [future] career. Others will tell you that children with computers at home do better in school. Even young children."

Do you really *need* a computer? Not necessarily. If you just have a vague sense that somehow you should have one because . . . well, you just should, then think again. Most of these machines are far from cheap. You don't need one to balance your checkbook (although many programs are sold to do just that). In fact, a pen, a piece of paper, and a pocket calculator will help you get the job done much quicker. Nor should you be swayed by the colorful patterns a computer can create on a TV screen: you are likely to stay interested in them no longer than you would want to gaze into a kaleidoscope.

Fun and Games

Not that fun wouldn't be a good reason to purchase a computer. There is a wide variety of game software available for every machine aimed at the home market—enough to provide countless hours of enjoyment for you and your children. In fact, arcade and home video games have replaced the movies as America's most popular mass diversion (aside from television, of course).

Video games have come a long way from Pong (the black and white tennis-type game that started the craze in the mid-1970s) to Pac-Man, Donkey Kong, and their cohorts. Space Invaders, which appeared in 1978, was the first of the loud, colorful, and immensely profitable games that are still with us. In these games, the movement of the various monsters and flying objects on the screen is controlled both by a predetermined sequence in the game's program and by a random number generator in the computer which governs which way an object will move and how fast it will go. Players use "joysticks" (often optional equipment on personal computers, but costing only about $10 each) to move objects around on the screen; technically, they are interacting with the game's program by inputting information to change the coordinates of the objects on the grid display.

Some of the more recently published game software is clearly aimed at the adult market. In a game called Dallas, according to the computer magazine *BYTE*, "The processor, when playing the role of J.R., has been programmed to cheat, lie and blackmail. . . ." The game Abuse will "call you something you've never been called before," promises its manufacturer. Tax Man will help you act out a veritable nightmare as an IRS agent pursues you across a giant Form 1040. According to *Time* magazine, in Softporn (available from On-Line Systems in California) "players seek to seduce three women, while avoiding hazards such as getting killed by a bouncer in a disco." (There is already considerable demand for a women's version.) There is even a program called Interlude which will give you sexual advice. When you run it the computer queries you on your mood and proclivities and responds with an agenda of things to do.

Computers as Educational Tools

Since having at least some knowledge of these machines is becoming imperative in our society, developing computer literacy is another good reason to buy a computer. But for just learning something about programming or how computer hardware works, the least expensive machines are perfectly adequate.

For more general educational purposes, a computer can be useful too. Computer-aided instruction (also known as CAI) has been used by industry and schools for some time now to train workers and students in specific subject areas. Everything from chemistry to German can be taught at a self-regulated pace through drill and review techniques. PLATO, one of the more popular series of CAI programs, is now being adapted for home machines.

LOGO, educational software which has been available for microcomputers since 1979, has begun to revolutionize the use of the computer for teaching. At first confined to the classroom, it is now available in versions for Apple, Atari, and Texas Instruments personal computers and could be the reason why many thousands of parents will buy one of these machines for their children.

This program emphasizes the interaction between the child and the machine, not just the passive absorption of whatever is on the screen. It was developed by a Massachusetts Institute of Technology (MIT) team led by Seymour Papert, who is active in the field of artificial intelligence. Papert, a former colleague of educational theorist Jean Piaget, emphasizes the idea that most learning takes place without formal education—for example, that is how we learn to walk and speak. LOGO, then, is an attempt to extend this "experiential" learning to the classroom.

Children can use LOGO to teach themselves mathematical concepts. By means of simple commands, the child instructs the computer to draw figures on the screen. An instrument called a "turtle" connects the points; the whole procedure is known as turtle geometry. A child might create a polygon (a geometric figure) by "walking out" the shape first, then instructing the computer (through the keyboard, a joystick, or other input device) to draw lines that replicate his or her movements across the floor. If this information is insufficient to complete the polygon, the machine will respond: "POLY WANTS MORE DATA." Consultant Brian Harvey, who has worked with LOGO in the Boston area schools, comments: "Students learn a lot about learning and thinking by using the computer as a model of themselves as learners."

Business Applications

Anyone who runs a small business—whether at home, in a storefront, or in an office suite—is a prime candidate for buying a personal computer. Software for accounts payable and receivable, general ledger, inventory, data storage, graphics, word processing, or calculating is readily available. But while games and other programs aimed at the home market tend to cost about $30 or less, business software is considerably more expensive: it is not unusual to spend several hundred dollars on one program.

Even for business applications the purchase of a computer should not be an automatic one. Does the quantity of paperwork justify spending $3,000 to $10,000 to put together a useful business system? Word processing—by which text can be electronically manipulated and stored, thus replacing the typewriter—might support the purchase of a computer if correspondence and reports flow steadily through your office. But a more moderate amount of writing could perhaps be handled just as expeditiously and more economically by a typist.

The personal computer is ideally suited for making sales and other business projections. The oft-imitated VisiCalc, the "electronic spreadsheet" program that helped propel Apple into its early dominant position in the personal computer industry, will store the numerical variables that contribute to a company's bottom line and will demonstrate the impact on all of those numbers of a change in any one of them. What if, for example, a company wanted to know the effect on its net profit of a possible increase in insurance rates (with optional plans, each of which could affect the business in different ways), an increase in the price of raw materials, a different way of handling inventory in accounting? The program automatically recalculates every other figure affected by that change, thus making it a very powerful planning tool.

Telecommunications

Buying a personal computer for its telecommunications capabilities may very well make sense. In addition to running programs that you buy or even write yourself, the personal computer also provides access to a whole world of information and services. All you do is dial a phone number. The vast data flow produced by our information-oriented society, once available only to large institutions via on-line database retrieval systems, is now available to you in your home on a reduced scale.

Teletext

The transmission of this type of data to the home has actually been going on for several years. Many cable television systems feature continuously changing printed displays of news, weather, and local events. Two British services originally took advantage of that part of the TV signal called the blanking interval (the black line you see between frames when the picture rolls vertically) to transmit over regular channels information that is then deciphered by means of a special attachment to the TV set. CBS and NBC are now in the process of introducing this system, generically known as teletext, into this country.

Videotex

Videotex (no "t" at the end) is something else again. This is an interactive system that allows the user to specify which kind of information is desired to respond to that information. Banking or shopping at home, as well as responding to questions posed by political pollsters are common applications. A modem connects the user's telephone to either a dedicated computer device supplied by the service or the user's own personal computer.

The British Post Office's Prestel, a service offered through home television, was begun in 1979 and was the first videotex system to go on line. Since then, several companies in this country have experimented with interactive TV. AT&T is known to have an interest in tapping its potential, and Warner Communications'

QUBE system has been offered to a limited number of households in Columbus, Ohio for several years now.

Information Services

Of the various suppliers of information to the home through personal computers, three most resemble the corporate-oriented data banks. These are The Source, CompuServe, and the Dow Jones News/Retrieval Service. To access them you need, besides a personal computer, a modem and some software. The data is transmitted by means of a packet-switching network you hook up to with a local telephone call.

Through The Source, owned by *Reader's Digest* and based in Virginia, more than twenty thousand subscribers can get current news summaries, Associated Press stories, stock quotes, movie reviews, and information on the status of legislation in the U.S. Congress. Electronic bulletin boards focusing on specific areas of interest allow users to ''post'' messages to all other subscribers and to receive responses as well. Private messages protected by code can be sent to a specific person on the Source network for the bargain rate of about five cents for every two paragraphs. There is an initial hookup fee of $100; hourly rates begin at $5.75 and vary with the time of day the service is accessed.

CompuServe, owned by H&R Block, is also inexpensive. In addition to information similar to that provided by The Source, CompuServe offers video games, sophisticated graphics, and consumer services such as shopping at home. Subscribers can even purchase software and have it transferred directly to their computer over the telecommunications line. The CompuServe service can be subscribed to at many Radio Shack stores or through CompuServe.

Dow Jones News/Retrieval, besides offering the obvious securities price information, also provides excerpts from the *Wall Street Journal* and *Barron's* as well as in-depth corporate data on more than six thousand companies, movie reviews, and up-to-the-minute sports information. Non-prime-time rates begin at fifteen cents a minute; over fifty thousand people are already on line.

Personal computers can do more than just receive information from these services. Software is now available, for example, for accessing large quantities of financial data at rapid speeds. Network connection time is therefore minimized; the information is stored in the computer and can be viewed at the user's leisure. Other programs can automatically evaluate stock quotes and integrate them into an established database—to update a stock portfolio, for example.

To Buy or Not To Buy

If you still feel that your needs justify the outlay of hundreds or possibly thousands of dollars on a personal computer, you must do some homework. The first thing you should do is decide which programs will be most helpful to you and then take a close look at the machines that will run them. Software is the key to getting the computer to do what you want it to do: if you buy the very best machine on the market and there is no software available to make it work for you, it won't amount to much.

Software compatibility from one machine to another should never be assumed. If you own an Apple and your neighbors have a Radio Shack TRS-80, you can't borrow that intriguing program they bought because it won't run on your machine. The crucial factor is the computer's operating system—the program either found in the read only memory (ROM) or transferred from disk into main memory each time the machine is used, and which enables the computer to manage input and output devices, organize files of information, and execute programs.

CP/M (Control Program for Microcomputers) is the closest thing to a standard operating system, and a good deal of sophisticated business software has been written for it. But many popular personal computers—such as the ones from Apple, Radio Shack, and Commodore—do not come with CP/M, and it can cost several hundred dollars to add the system.

When it comes to buying the machine itself, make sure you are reasonably well informed before talking to the computer store salespeople, who usually work on commission and may not be thoroughly familiar with the machines or software they sell.

Stores that charge list price (or close to it) will often stress the support they offer after the sale. Whether you will be able to rely on this support can be determined by inquiring about a particular store's reputation. Mail-order houses offer substantial discounts but due to the nature of the sale can offer little or no real support.

Talk to people who own personal computers. There's nothing like a recommendation from someone who's bought one and is happy with it. Read the articles, reviews, and advertisements in the computer magazines (*Personal Computing* and *Popular Computing* are good places to start); they will give you a sense of which machines have comparable features and at what cost. Since this industry is changing so rapidly, books you find at the library are likely to be out of date. But most bookstores are now flooded with paperbacks about personal computers, and many of these will give you a detailed brand-by-brand comparison. Two of the best are by Peter McWilliams: *The Word Processing Book* and *The Personal Computer Book*.

Once you know what your software needs are, the next decision you will have to make (aside from which brand to buy) is how much memory you will need. Anything above 1K will suffice if you just want to learn BASIC and write short, simple programs. For most home applications 16K to 32K should be enough, although many game programs written for the popular Apple require more. If your computer is going to be used for serious business applications, 48K is the minimum necessary amount. In businesses where quick access to a large volume of records is required, 128K, 256K, or even more may be needed, and the purchase of a Winchester (hard) disk drive (at $1,500 or more) would be in order.

The Total Package

As when buying a stereo system or video tape recorder, you're not necessarily through once you have purchased the basic equipment. A keyboard (or pressure pad substitute), central processing unit, and internal memory come with every unit, but you may have to supply your own video display. That could be your TV, or a monochrome or color monitor costing several hundred dollars, if you want to draw high-resolution graphics. Business users generally opt for a screen with green letters because they supposedly lead to less eye strain, although amber is gaining popularity.

In the less expensive machines such as the Timex Sinclair 1000 and VIC-20, common monaural cassette recorders costing about $60 apiece are usually used for secondary memory. But floppy disks, which can store large quantities of data and retrieve programs quickly, are usually used with the better machines. Disk drives cost about $500 apiece; the disks themselves, when bought in quantities of ten or more, can usually be had for two to five dollars each. For applications such as word processing, at least two drives are preferred. Word processing also requires the purchase of a printer—preferably of better quality. The best printers go for over $1,500, but Smith Corona recently introduced one that, although relatively slow (120 words per minute), can be bought for about $650. Dot matrix printers, good for applications other than word processing, start at a few hundred dollars.

Modems begin at slightly over $100 for the one that goes with VIC-20 and can range up to several hundred dollars each. A perusal of computer magazine advertisements will give a good sense of other available optional equipment, some of it quite exotic. Examples are the $600 Armdroid robot arm, which is sensitive enough to pick up an egg without breaking it, and the Votrax Type 'N Talk, which for about $300 will give your digital servant a voice. In some cases, peripheral equipment requires additional interface circuitry costing several hundred dollars.

If you are buying a total system and not just the bare-bones computer, it will, obviously, be reflected in the price you pay. You will be paying more, but you may be able to get a package discount. The Radio Shack Model III, for example, can be purchased with 16K of internal memory and a cassette recorder for off-line programs and data storage for about $1,000. But the same machine with two disk drives, 48K of memory, a letter-quality printer for word processing, and a modem for telecommunications will cost at least $4,000.

Choosing A Personal Computer

The following brief consumers' guide is meant to provide general guidance only. The prices assume a certain amount of discounting and if they change they will probably decrease due to technological improvements and increasing competition. The features offered by each manufacturer are likely to be even more impressive by the time you read this.

Game Systems and Pocket Computers

Dedicated computer modules whose single-mindedness is devoted to video games are often priced under $200. The **Atari Video Computer Systems** lead in this market with Mattel's **Intellivision**, and Magnavox's **Odyssey** and **Colecovision** giving chase. The games are contained in cartridges which sell for about $30 each and are plugged into the machine, which in turn is attached to your TV to provide a video display. These systems are actually extensions of your television—somewhat intricate electronic toys, although newer models can be upgraded into full-fledged computers.

Hand-held pocket computers from manufacturers such as Panasonic and Hewlett Packard are more sophisticated than even the most advanced calculator. They generally have a few K of memory and are programmable in BASIC. But they lack CRT screens and their visual displays are usually limited to one brief line. The amount of software for these machines (usually available in cards) is not extensive, and they are most often used by scientists and engineers who deal exclusively with numbers. A $250 off-the-shelf Hewlett Packard HP-41, as a matter of fact, has been used by astronauts aboard the space shuttle.

Inexpensive Machines

Computers in this category cost less than $500 and are aimed at nonbusiness users. They come without monitors but can be connected easily to a television set (obviously, you can't receive any broadcast programs while the computer is in use). Relatively inexpensive software is available for all these machines and in the cases of the VIC-20, Atari 400, and Texas Instruments TI 99/4A, can be had in the form of a cartridge that is simply placed into a slot in the computer.

There could be a $100 computer in your future—the **Timex Sinclair 1000.** Its measurements (6" × 6½" × 1½") and weight (all of twelve ounces) probably make this little gem the only personal computer you could misplace. True, it comes with only 2K of memory, has a pressure pad instead of a keyboard, and lacks color, but it's like the talking dog that astounds you even with its limited vocabulary. This computer is ideal as a starter—to learn BASIC and then see if you might want to go on to bigger and more expensive machines. It attaches to your television and for an additional $50 you can plug in a module that brings it up to 16K. A somewhat more expensive color version with movable keys should be available by the time you read this.

The company that once brought you James Cagney and Edward G. Robinson is now making another fortune with Pac-Man, the little creature that eats dots. In 1976, Warner Communications (Warner Brothers in a simpler time) bought Atari for a bargain $28 million. "Atari" means "go" in Japanese, and go it has—its current yearly gross is approaching $2 billion. Although there have been some less-than-favorable reviews of the version of Pac-Man made available for Atari's Video Computer System, the edition produced for Atari's personal computers has been well received—and in either case, the cash has been flowing in.

Atari computers should not be confused with the company's video game player. The **Atari 400** personal computer sells for about $275 and has a pressure pad instead of a conventional keyboard, which means that you press down on a plastic membrane instead of a key or button: this feature enables Atari to keep the price down, but not everybody is comfortable with it. The Atari 400 is known for its superb color graphics and sound and it comes with slots for plug-in Atari game cartridges, a wide variety of which are now available (BASIC, incidentally, does not come with the computer; it must be purchased as an option).

The **Atari 800** is the same machine as the 400 except for a typewriterlike keyboard and an internal memory of 48K. Although its discounted price is about $600—which ordinarily would put it in the business computer league—it is not likely to be found in a business setting; it is most often used to play games and run the type of home-oriented software available for low-priced computers.

Commodore, a company that until a year or two ago had concentrated on more expensive machines, has made a big splash with its **VIC-20,** a $175 computer. Like the Atari 400, it accepts cartridges—although not the Atari cartridges—but unfortunately there are not nearly as many cartridges available for the VIC-20 as for the Atari. It comes with 5K expand-

The Atari 800, which has a standard keyboard. The Atari 400 has a pressure pad instead of a regular keyboard; a bell rings to indicate that you have pressed down hard enough to register the character.

able to 32K, the peripheral equipment available for it is inexpensive, and it has good color and sound.

The **Radio Shack Color Computer** has gotten good reviews but until recently was hampered by two factors: it was sold only in Radio Shack stores and software for it was scarce. As these conditions are remedied and the price drops, this computer may really make its mark. Prices start in the $350 range for 16K and reach about $600 for 32K with a more complex and powerful version of BASIC.

The **Texas Instruments Home Computer** (TI99/4A) is priced like Radio Shack's Color Computer but may have an edge in the features it offers. Unlike the Radio Shack machine, it takes cartridges, is expandable to 52K, and offers a more diverse selection of software (including a version of LOGO). Television and print advertising featuring Bill Cosby has helped boost this personal computer up to the best-seller category.

Medium-Priced
Personal Computers

Machines priced between $500 and $1,500 can be found in both the home and at the office. They are still rather high-priced machines for playing games but often have stunning graphics and are sophisticated and powerful enough to run business software. In a business setting they frequently utilize a variety of peripheral equipment (at the minimum, a good dot matrix or letter-quality printer); the final cost of such a system can run well over $5,000.

Of all the personal computers, **Apple** is probably the best known. The first Apple was built in a garage in Palo Alto, California, by two young Californians, Steven Wozniak and Steve Jobs. The sprightly pair priced their first model at $666.66, and their company slogan was "Don't trust any computer you can't lift." Apple's friendly, unintimidating image was enhanced by some cleverly prepared television commercials a few years later featuring the cool presence of Dick Cavett.

The flagship of the Apple Line, as this is written, is the Apple IIe, which sells for about $1,300 (you supply the monitor or attach it to a television set). It has 64K of internal memory and good color graphics, but its main claim to fame is its software (all of it on disk), a larger and more varied collection of programs than that written for any other personal computer. A $125 adapter enables it to display 80 characters per line on a screen, thus imitating the appearance of a piece of typing paper and making the machine useful for word processing.

Where Apple surged ahead by dint of smart public relations and a timely link-up with some crucial software, Radio Shack achieved its own preeminence because of the nationwide distribution power of thousands of company stores and franchised dealers. Its **TRS-80 Model III** now competes with the Apple. This Radio Shack machine comes with a built-in black and white monitor, and in various configurations from 16K memory and no disk drive to 48K with two drives. Prices range from about $900 to $2,500.

The no-nonsense, businesslike appearance of these computers suggests the use to which they are often put. They are found in accountants' offices, on the desks of corporate managers, even on farms or in beauty parlors—almost anywhere a reliable, reasonably priced, solidly built personal computer can be of use. Only the Apple has more software published for it.

Commodore, an early competitor of Apple and Radio Shack for the school market, now has personal computers in all price categories. Its **PET** line, which has been around for about five years, is price competitive with the Apple IIe and Radio Shack TRS-80 Model III. PETs have built-in monitors, do not offer color, and display varying numbers of characters per line depending on the particular model.

The recently introduced **Commodore 64** should not only give Apple and Radio Shack a run for their money, but also may create some problems for Atari.

The Radio Shack TRS-80 Model III. To the right of the built-in black and white screen are slots for two optional disk drives.

This machine aims to be all things to all people. It has the 64K of memory its name indicates, excellent color, and superb sound that has already been compared to that emanating from the best synthesizers. The CP/M operating system, which enables the machine to run a whole slew of business programs, is available as a plug-in option; there is even a slot for slipping in a game cartridge when the business day is over. This compact unit resembles the lower-priced VIC-20 and will fit into a briefcase. Its already low list price of $595 can be found discounted to as little as $475.

Business Machines

Machines in this category come with at least 64K of internal memory, sometimes expandable to as much as 1,000K or more. Video displays of 80 characters per line for 24 lines are standard. Since these computers will usually handle several different types of jobs—accounting, record keeping and word processing, for example—they are likely to be purchased as part of a package that includes a good deal of expensive software and at least a few pieces of optional equipment such as a printer and a modem.

Photo courtesy of IBM Corporation

The memory capacity of the IBM Personal Computer is expandable to 1,000K. There is room for two optional disk drives in the unit below the screen. The printer, left, is also optional.

One business-oriented machine—the **IBM Personal Computer**—has outpaced all others in the publicity it has received, and this is reflected in its rapidly increasing sales figures. IBM introduced the Personal Computer in the autumn of 1981. For approximately

$3,700 (64K, two disk drives, and an excellent monitor), how good is the IBM Personal Computer? Very good—and it will get even better as more software and peripheral equipment become available for it. It is expandable to 1,000K and contains a 16-bit microprocessor, a feature likely to become standard in the better business-oriented personal computers. Sixteen-bit machines work faster and can store more information than 8-bit computers. The IBM Personal Computer's color graphics are also excellent.

The **Apple III,** which retails for about three thousand dollars, comes with 128K of memory (which can even be doubled), and a built-in disk drive. The first Apple IIIs had more bugs than an unscreened porch on a summer's night, but those have been eliminated. This computer does not come with a monitor, although that and a starting package of software are often included in special sales. A big advantage of this machine is that it can run much of the plentiful software written for the cheaper Apple IIe.

Radio Shack has designed two computers for the business market, the **Model II** and the **Model 16.** The Model II, priced at or about $3,000 and soon to be replaced by the slightly more advanced Model 12, comes with 64K of memory that can be expanded to 256K, an 8" disk drive, and a built-in monitor with white characters on a black background. The Model 16 features two microprocessors, one a 16-bit (software for this is just starting to appear) and the other an 8-bit to run programs currently available for the Model II. This computer comes with a green screen, 128K of memory expandable to 512K, and a double-capacity 8" disk drive. The price of the Model 16 is about $5,000.

Portability is already a feature in the maturing personal computer industry, as it is in radio, television, and stereo components. The **Osborne 1,** the first of the "take-it-with-you" machines, created a great stir when it was introduced in 1981. For $2,000 you get a real package of goodies: a 64K computer with two disk drives *and* $1,500 worth of software, including the popular WORD STAR word processing program, a spread sheet, and two kinds of BASIC. This personal computer weighs less than 24 pounds, fits under an airplane seat, and may be used with an optional battery pack. Unfortunately, its built-in black and white screen measures a meager 5 inches and can display only 52 characters per line. Extensive use of the Osborne might necessitate the purchase of an external monitor.

A number of other portable computers have appeared recently; one of them is challenging the Osborne for market supremacy. The **Kaypro II** has a 9" screen with full 80-character display, costs $1,795, and comes with a software package similar to the Osborne's. Where the Osborne is often purchased as a second computer, the Kaypro II frequently ends up being the only machine for its growing number of users.

By now the business market is crowded with many brands of personal computers. Among them are Altos, Cromemco, Digital Equipment, North Star, Vector, and Xerox (whose Model 820, some in the company had hoped, would become the "worm" that ate the Apple). And then there are the Japanese machines. Apple's quotable Steve Jobs predicts that they will "flop up on the shore like dead fish." Maybe. But one could imagine Chrysler and General Motors executives saying the same of Japanese autos not long ago.

Fragile:
Handle with Care

If you buy a personal computer, treat it with kid gloves. Personal computers are not indestructible. "These damned [personal] computer systems break; they break a lot," writes Wayne Green, editor of *Desktop Computing*. This is especially true of components such as printers and disk drives, which have moving parts.

Generally speaking, personal computers and people alike function best under the same conditions: moderate temperature and humidity and a low level of dust. A floppy disk should be treated as if it were a phonograph record: kept away from heat and stored upright in its jacket (it stays on when you insert the disk into the drive); and its surface should never be touched. (For some strange reason, incidentally, ads and brochures for personal computers often show someone beside the machine courting disaster with a cup at his or her elbow.)

Program Pirates

One problem that has plagued phonograph record companies has already become a serious one for producers of personal computer software. Record companies lose immense sums when people tape copies of friends' records rather than buy their own. All it takes to hoist the skull and crossbones is a disk drive to play and copy.

Some software publishers have sought to protect themselves by making purchasers agree in writing to be legally liable for unauthorized duplication of programs.

Often software is encrypted to prevent copying. But as you might imagine, people who are really involved with computers are not going to be stopped by that. Two programs, Locksmith and Nibbles Away 2, costing under $100 each, are capable of picking apart most security codes. What, you might ask, prevents *these* two programs from being pirated? Well, they've already been revised several times to keep them ahead of larcenous transcribers and they have their own protection codes—although the distributor of Locksmith now says he's going to take the code off his software because he's "sick and tired of being called a hypocrite."

CHAPTER 9

THE COMPUTER IN YOUR LIFE

Although today most people accept the fact that computers influence their lives—or may even fear that their lives may one day be controlled by them—they may still be unaware of just how closely their daily activities are tied to these machines. When things go along as usual, we haven't much reason to be aware of behind-the-scenes changes such as our daily newspaper converting from hot- to cold-type production methods. And because these changes are quiet—sometimes seemingly insidious—they can often make the impact of the computer seem far less powerful than it actually is.

It's All in a Computerized Day

But these days there is a computer behind almost every button we push, every thing we buy—indeed, just about every product and service we use from the hour we are awakened by a microprocessor-controlled clock radio to the moment we turn out the last light at night, thus temporarily cutting our ties to the computer-monitored and -switched utility company.

Without computer calculations, that weather forecast you rely on in the morning wouldn't be so reliable. The car you drive to work probably contains a microprocessor to insure maximum fuel efficiency and minimum air pollution; it was almost certainly manufactured by computer-controlled robots. Even the traffic lights you encounter are probably controlled by computers.

Your office is an automated world of word processing and other forces of electronic communication. The hamburger you eat for lunch may have been cooked with the aid of a computer, and the animal from which it came was probably bred with advice and genetic analysis from a data processor. The book or newspaper you read in the remaining minutes of your lunch hour was set by computer in "cold type." And the get-well card you almost forgot to buy is for a hospitalized friend who has probably been monitored by several computerized machines from the moment he set foot in the institution.

Groceries you pick up on the way home may be inventoried and checked out with the aid of a computerized point-of-sale terminal; the cash you buy them with is dispensed by an automated-teller machine. And the so-called "junk mail" awaiting you at home is the product of computerized mailing lists; you receive bills that have been processed and printed by computer and a magazine with that funny-looking computer-coded label. The calls you make in the evening are switched by . . . guess what? Even your stereo, if it was purchased within the last few years, most likely contains one or more microprocessors.

Around the house there are all kinds of other electronic consumer goods which contain microprocessors, or "computers-on-a-chip." These small, cheap chips will fit into almost anything and can program appliances to perform any series of functions in any sequence. When linked to a timing device, these automated activities can even take place while you are away (the videocassette recorder and telephone answering device for example, make use of the capabilities).

The last straw is Junior, who's had access to personal computers in school since the first grade. Two of his friends have them at home, a third is about to get one. Now *he* must have one, too—"for educational purposes"—not to mention for playing video games. (That last is a powerful argument because it just might keep him from hanging out in the video game arcades, his generation's mesmerizing version of the corner candy store.)

Word Processors: A Revolution In Office Technology

Even if you can't afford a computer for your own home use, you may very well have one in your office. In the workaday world, computers are becoming as commonplace as pencil sharpeners. The traditional bases of office technology—the typewriter, telephone, filing cabinet, and stamp and envelope—are undergoing a transformation. All their functions are being brought together into a single electronic system accessible from each "work station" (what used to be your desk and chair) and tied into telecommunications lines, so that everyone is just a push-button away from everyone else.

The word processor is already a fact of life in many offices where "keyboarding" has replaced typ-

The Xerox 860 information processing system combines a word processor and a general business computer in one machine. The printer at the rear is included in the system.

ing. This machine resembles the typewriter only in the way the copy is initially entered. After the first draft is typed, words, phrases, paragraphs, or whole pages can be deleted, moved around, or split up, and then dispersed throughout a business letter, contract, or book-length manuscript. Proofreading and revising is done on the screen. There is no longer any need for correcting fluid; retyping an entire document is a thing of the past. Perhaps most importantly, the entire document can also be stored on disk for future revisions or printouts of the data it contains.

The word processor is far more flexible than typewriter and paper can ever be. Forms can be redesigned and lengthy documents automatically prepared on the machine. "Boilerplate" phrases that are often used intact (for example, in legal documents) can be stored in the word processor's memory and then called up and inserted whenever needed.

Some word processors even enable you to do electronic cutting and pasting by displaying text from two different documents on a split screen. Words can be removed from one document and inserted at a specified spot in the other. The processor's "dictionary" can hyphenate words at the end of a line, and the carriage return automatically moves to the beginning of the next line.

If you're not sure how to spell a word and don't want to stop what you're doing to find out, you can mark each use of the word with a symbol. Then, when you have determined the correct spelling, you enter it once and use a special command to automatically insert it, correctly spelled, throughout the document. The built-in dictionaries are also used to correct misspellings by scanning the text and highlighting words that appear to contain mistakes. According to a recent *Science* article there is even a program that will point an accusing finger at "split infinitives, clichés, excessive use of passive voice, sexist phrases and a variety of other flaws."

These machines are not as expensive as you might think: excellent dedicated word processors that can be had from IBM, Wang, or Lanier cost not much more than $6,000. A perfectly serviceable system based on a personal computer, software, and a letter-quality printer can be purchased for under $5,000—and it can of course be used for anything else a computer does, with the help of the appropriate software.

Electronic Filing And Mail

Interconnection is the byword of the automated office. Much of the information that was once put into manila folders in metal filing cabinets (statistics, lists) can now be stored on computer disk or tape and can be made accessible to any work station in the company whose occupant is authorized to tap the company database. Terminals and word processors can also be used to transmit text (memos, for example) to any other machine linked to the office network, whether it is in that office or one thousand miles away: thus we have electronic mail. In on-line teleconferences, participants can consider the comments of others, displayed on their CRT screens, before entering their own remarks. Company documents can even be written and edited by different people in different cities through the linking of word processors and telecommunication devices.

Computer Journalism

A revolution in the print media has been brought about by the combination of word processing, database retrieval systems, image manipulation on a CRT screen, and telecommunications technology. *Time* magazine adopted computerized typesetting in 1967; in 1979 it boasted that its system could correctly hyphenate 14-syllable words, set type in any of 127 fonts, tailor-fit copy to a layout, draw boxes and assorted rules, and, at the rate of one page every 15 seconds, whisk the whole magazine off to press via telephone lines.

Until about ten years ago, the newsroom of your favorite daily could easily have resembled something out of the 1930s, with rows of desks, old typewriters, and copy boys scurrying about. The reporter's copy was hand-delivered to the editor, corrected, and then dispatched to the Linotype operators. The text was cast into hot lead type from which galley proofs were run off. Corrected type went to the composing room for page makeup; approved pages were then made into plates for the giant presses. Along the way there was ink enough to smudge everybody's hands.

Today's journalist, on the other hand, is a reporter-typesetter. Stories are typed on terminal keyboards instead of battered Underwoods and are sent into electronic storage. An editor revises the copy on another CRT screen. Final copy is automatically printed out in "repro" (photographically reproducible) form; commercial artists prepare mechanicals for printing by the photo-offset method. If the actual printing is to be done elsewhere, microwaves bounced off satellites can convey each page to any remote location. Even the reporter on a distant assignment can use a small portable terminal which stores up to 20,000 words. Copy is phoned in via modem, without a word ever appearing on a piece of paper.

■ ▬ ▪▪ ▀▀▀ ▪ ▌▬ ▬ ▬ ▌▀▀▀ ▄▪▌■

Utility Billing

Computers perform a wide variety of functions for utilities' billing purposes: record keeping, information accessing, calculating, and document preparation are routinely assigned to the computers by gas, telephone, and electric companies. What consumers hope is that they perform those tasks correctly. Inherently high rates have nothing to do with the computer, but if an individual bill seems inordinately steep, an error might have been made, although probably not by the machine. Someone else may have been charging calls to your phone or the meter-reader may have made a very human error, and the computer obligingly passed it along.

The handling of your bill as well as the organization and storage of your account information are routine computerized procedures. Although considerably larger than most other utility companies, Con Edison (the company that supplies electricity to the New York City metropolitan area) is a fairly accurate model of the kind of company that probably serves you. Con Edison generates bills using batch processing methods; customer inquiries are handled by an on-line da-

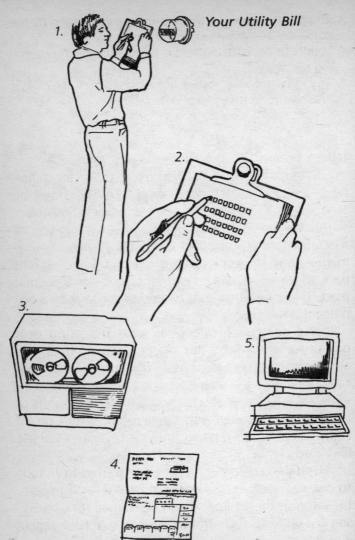

Your Utility Bill
1. *Your meter is read.*
2. *The figures are marked on an optical character recognition form.*

3. *The form is scanned, the information is checked by the computer and it is then stored on tape.*
4. *Your bill is generated from the tape by the batch processing method.*
5. *The information is copied onto a disk, from which it is available for answering queries on line.*

tabase system.

When a Con Ed employee reads an electric meter, he or she marks the figures on a form which will be scanned by an optical character recognition machine. Within twenty-four hours of the meter reading this information is transferred to tape; an "if/then" branch in the program automatically compares the current data to the past usage and kicks out for a second reading any numbers that exceed past usage by a significant amount.

The computer calculates your bill using programmed formulas for the rate per kilowatt hour, fuel adjustments, taxes, etc. The machine then automatically prints out and addresses the bill; it can also print a message to thank you for your prompt payments or to encourage you to be more prompt. The Con Ed invoice is printed on paper, but many utilities still use IBM cards.

Updated customer files are transferred from tape to disk for storage; this information is directly accessible through the on-line system developed for Con Edison by IBM. This enormous system supports almost 2,000 terminals throughout the New York City metropolitan area; Con Ed employees can display a customer's account information within three seconds of typing in a query.

Electronic Banking

Like the utility companies, banks have for a number of years relied on their computers to process checks, calculate interest on savings or loans, and prepare monthly statements. Now, banks in most major cities and many outlying areas as well offer a remarkable new computerized service which is radically changing our economic and monetary habits: the automated-teller machine.

Originally introduced in 1970, these machines supplement the network of credit cards already embedded in our economic system, and they have not been cheap to implement: New York's Citibank spent $175 million to develop its system and put it on line—$40 million for the software alone.

Bank customers can withdraw money, make deposits or payments, or transfer money between accounts at any hour at one of these automated tellers, just by pushing buttons, entering a secret personal code number, and inserting a plastic card that usually contains a magnetic strip with a code that is read and checked by the computer. Minicomputers at the bank's central processing location keep a "memo file" of all machine transactions made during the day and can set a limit on how much a customer can withdraw in any twenty-four hour period. At the close of the business day the data is transferred to the bank's mainframe computer, where it is stored (and from where your monthly statement is generated).

Banks actually began to transfer funds by wire in

1950, when Western Union's teletype network linked 142 institutions together. Since the late 1960s, sentiment has grown within the industry for a standardized system of electronic funds transfer (EFT). Ultimately this will completely do away with checks and will decrease the need for real currency as well. Your employer, for example, could send payroll information to the bank on tape; you would never see a paycheck. Point-of-sale devices in every store could be tied into the banking system via telecommunications lines so your purchases could be charged against your account electronically.

So far the idea has been slow to take hold except on some preliminary experimental bases; this may be due in part to consumers' reluctance to give up cancelled checks as receipts. And there is also a fear of electronic thievery.

One legal problem that must be dealt with before EFT can become a widespread reality is the clarification of statutes dealing with branch banks, which are strictly regulated under current law. In a totally wired banking system, what is a "branch" bank? A few years ago, a Nebraska supermarket chain was taken to court when it installed machines that enabled shoppers to pay for their groceries by automatically transferring funds from their bank account to the store's. The contention was that the store was operating as an unregulated branch of the bank, but the court disagreed.

Airline Reservation Systems

Airline reservation systems have been in operation since the early 1960s, freeing many travel agents from what was once a heavy burden of paperwork. They arrange for space on flights and facilitate car rentals and hotel reservations as well. When an agent calls up the inventory of a flight on the terminal, the central computer tells when each reservation was made, the number of people in each party and their names, whether a reservation is confirmed, standby, or cancelled—and, of course, provides a running account of seats available in each class.

This system is far from perfect: there are in fact a number of competing airlines with computerized reservation systems rather than one unified network for the entire industry. Today about forty percent of all computerized travel agencies use American Airlines' Sabre system, the industry's pioneer; it provides access to reservation information, schedules, and booking procedures for *all* airlines.

Air Traffic Control

Your personal safety in the air (as well as the efficiency of your air travel) is the direct result of the computer's ability to store, analyze, compare, and disseminate critical information regarding air traffic activity and weather patterns. Computers make navigational calculations and monitor the plane's intricate flight systems. Equipment aboard each plane automatically transmits altitude and other data to one of twenty control centers throughout the country, where it is instantly displayed on a radar screen. When the computer detects two planes drawing dangerously close, an alert message is flashed on the screen.

Outwitting the Weather

Weather forecasts are probably more vital to airline pilots than to the rest of us, but they *are* of concern to anybody who plans to go out during the day. In recent years, long-range weather forecasting has become increasingly based on complicated mathematical models of weather systems. These models—important tools in the physical and social sciences—simulate real conditions and processes by representing them in a series of mathematical formulas and equations. If the quantitative models are accurate descriptions of real conditions and the data are also accurate, the system should be able to predict future events accurately too.

Computers used in scientific research have made it possible to build models that simulate complex events involving large numbers or great magnitudes. Astronomer Richard Miller, for example, has created a computer model of the evolution of galaxies, which involves millions of calculations. He uses a sophisticated computer to plot the location of 100,000 points, each of which stands for a large number of the billions of stars in a galaxy. The machine's calculations are used to produce an animated film that shows in a minute what took place over millions of years.

For long-range weather forecasts, temperature, humidity, barometric pressure, and wind velocity data are needed from many locations, over a period of time. When the forecasting model was first developed in the early twentieth century, it took so long to process all the numbers that the result was retroactive predictions. Number-crunching computers and satellite photos have corrected that, made predictions far more accurate, and speeded up forecasters' response time in crisis situations (for example, hurricanes). Computers also compare forecasts against the latest reported readings and then update the predictions, so a radio announcer is less likely now to announce sunshine on a rainy day.

The National Weather Service is currently putting on line a $16 million computer that will process data from 100,000 local stations and report the results twice a day. This larger machine will accommodate more data to create better weather models—an essential element in helping us function more comfortably and safely in our daily lives.

Medical Applications

These modeling systems play a vital role in all branches of scientific research and its intricate applications, not the least of which is medical diagnosis.

The computer's ability to run programs with simple "if/then" branches can often save lives in hospital intensive care units. Sensing devices attached to patients are hooked up to computers which monitor the instrument readings; if the figures exceed those written into the program some sort of alarm is sounded. In 1979 a computer-monitoring system installed at North Shore University Hospital on Long Island was credited with cutting the in-hospital heart attack mortality rate by almost fifty percent.

Probably no other computer application in medicine has gotten as much publicity as computerized axial tomography—the CAT scan. Far too expensive for every hospital to have but greatly desired for the prestige it confers, the CAT scan has become a prime tool in diagnosing conditions that previously would have necessitated exploratory surgery. Essentially, it cuts with a beam of atomic particles rather than a scalpel to produce a cross-sectional image.

An X-ray machine rotates around the patient to produce a sequence of images which are then processed by the computer to create a three-dimensional picture. Without a computer to enhance the images, those pictures would not have a high enough resolution to be useful; but what was once an unidentifiable shadow on film can now be identified with reasonable certainty.

The positron emission tomography scanner, or PET scan, is used in a similar fashion to analyze the body's metabolism. Brain disorders, for example, can be diagnosed by monitoring the metabolism of radioactive glucose. The PET scan is therefore especially useful in examining stroke victims, since various body movements are controlled by different parts of the brain, each of which metabolizes at different rates.

Researchers also hope to use this machine to learn more about heart disease by studying the way that the heart and blood vessels break down glucose; and about cancer, since malignant cells metabolize glucose at higher rates than normal cells. Unfortunately, the PET scan costs millions of dollars and there are only about twenty in this country to date.

In another medical application, computers are used to analyze and refine the images produced by the probing sound waves sent out by ultrasound devices. These machines, which are particularly useful for examining moving targets such as the heart and the fetus, are based on the principle that different types of tissues have different acoustical properties and will thus reflect sound differently.

The most important medical application of the computer may well be diagnosis, wherein the computer compares relevant data on a variety of diseases that have been programmed in, with the symptoms from a particular case. Then, using a series of "if/then" comparisons, it narrows down the possibilities and comes up with a plausible diagnosis.

A computer program called Internist, developed at the University of Pittsburgh, contains data for more than 500 diseases which are cross-referenced to over 3,500 symptoms. Computer researchers at Stanford and Rutgers Universities, after observing doctors in action over a period of time, have devised PUFF, a program that produces highly accurate diagnoses in lung diseases, and ONCOCIN, a program capable of dealing with the subtle mix of therapies used to treat some forms of cancer.

William Baker of the National Institutes of Health stated in a *Time* magazine article that the University of

Pittsburgh's CADUCEUS program "would be a board-certified internist if it were human." The computer has limitless stamina and a reliable memory, fine attributes for a doctor. And because no physician can be expected to keep completely up to date with the deluge of data that emanates from our research institutions, the computer will increasingly serve as an auxiliary memory for the physician, simplifying the enormous task of keeping abreast of the literature.

Help for the Handicapped

When used as a tool to convert information from one form into another, the computer offers the handicapped an electronic path to a new realm of freedom. The blind can now "read," even if the book is not available in Braille or as part of their library's "talking" books program. In the late 1970s Ray Kurzweill, using an optical scanner and voice synthesizer linked to a computer, developed a machine that was capable of reading aloud books printed in any typeface. Whereas Braille takes years to master, the Kurzweill machine can be learned in one day. An initial price of $25,000 puts it out of the reach of most individuals, but some institutions are beginning to acquire them.

The deaf can now carry on telephone conversations with the aid of a modem and a CRT screen. The computer's ability to control anything in the house that can be operated by electricity has enabled the handicapped to gain control over a large part of their immediate environment. Even quadraplegics can open doors for themselves, metaphorically and literally, through ingenious techniques that have enabled them to use a computer keyboard.

Processed Politics

Word processing and the "relational database" have proved to be just the thing for members of Congress. Each representative in the House gets a computer allowance, most of which is used to send out a steady stream of replies to constituents' queries and complaints. Your legislator maintains a computerized file of "boilerplate" remarks on the issues of the day; by pressing a few buttons the relevant paragraphs can be slipped into a "personalized" letter. Then the recipient's name and address go into the database, where they are cross-referenced to the relevant subject; should the legislator want to make a related statement at a later date, it can be transmitted effortlessly to those who have already shown an interest in the matter.

American politics has already begun to show the effects of these practices. Single-issue groups have taken advantage of word processors and computer based mailing lists to get their messages across to select groups and galvanize them into action. The use of this process in fund raising has been honed into a fine art by Richard Viguerie and may have been an important element in Ronald Reagan's capture of the presidency in 1980.

Computer-Aided Design And Manufacturing

Computers have been used in industry for some time, and in recent years for completely automated production from design to fabrication. The use of computers in the manufacture of machine parts and finished goods is quite intricate and has had a great effect on the physical structure and social organization of the plants in which they have been installed.

Computer-aided design and computer-aided manufacturing— or CAD/CAM—is the ultimate in automation. The process moves from idea to finished product with very few hands getting dirty. As a matter of fact, there are not too many human hands involved at all. Blueprints need no longer be laboriously drawn and redrawn by draftsmen, since virtually anything that can be drawn on paper can be drawn on a CRT screen. It can then be stored in the computer's memory and called up for revision at any time, just like the text in a word processor.

Two different methods are used to create such drawings: the boundary representation method, by which the designer creates shapes on the screen by commanding the computer to connect a series of grid coordinates, and a second approach, often combined with boundary representation, in which standard "primitive" shapes are called up from the computer's memory and combined on the screen to create more complex forms.

Through CAD (Computer Aided Design), a product design can easily be created and modified on the computer screen and then stored for later use or further modification.

Before a computer-designed product can be manufactured, it must be tested for structural soundness. In the past this would have required the construction and destruction of one or more expensive physical prototypes. Not any more. Now this can be done by subjecting the design, still on the screen, to simulated tests in which the computer can gauge the real-life effect of an adverse condition on the finished product.

The automotive and aerospace industries are currently leading the way in introducing CAD and are also pioneering CAM. If increasingly higher levels of productivity are our economic aim, then the computer-directed, robot-operated production line is where we are headed. Ever since the Czech playwright Karel Čapek gave us the word robot from his native tongue's "robota" (meaning "forced labor"), it has conjured up images of powerful mechanical men, menacingly stalking the earth. In reality, robots tend to be all arm. Originally they were used in factories to "pick and place," automatically moving objects from one place to another according to a predetermined sequence.

Now, thanks to optical scanners and digitized TV pictures, robots are beginning to "see." This makes them capable of carrying out just about any production line task imaginable. Pushed to its logical extreme, this process (automation) could fill the factory with very smart machines and the streets with unemployed workers (more of this later).

In most cases computerized manufacturing has not pushed things to this point but even the half-way measures are precipitating vast changes for those employed in these industries. In the linear programming technique, for example, the computer is employed as an efficiency engineer. Everything from office and factory floor layout to the scheduling of the production process itself—including coffee breaks and lunch hours—has been analyzed to determine which combination of human and machine "inputs" would maximize profits.

Computers In the Humanities

Computers have been utilized in the humanities as well as in science and industry. Computerized textual analysis has been used in literary criticism and historical writing to solve problems of disputed authorship; political scientists have spotted trends in elections and legislative voting patterns that might otherwise have gone undetected. Archaeologists have established patterns in the location and quantity of objects found in some digs, and musicians employing synthesizers that mathematically manipulate tonal values have created some very intriguing new works.

Defense Applications

The computer has enhanced our ability to destroy as well as to design and create. Virtually every weapons system in use today contains a computer that calculates, navigates, or controls. Billions of dollars have been spent on software development to support defense-oriented hardware. The cruise missile, for example, contains a digitized map in its guidance system that enables the craft to make last-minute course changes as it homes in on its target. Ultimately, the United States Department of Defense hopes to have maps of the entire world digitized and programmed into a generation of "smart" weapons. There is even a new computer language, ADA, developed especially for defense applications.

The military recently drafted computerized animation—not unlike what the Walt Disney studios used to create the movie *TRON*—for its own interactive applications. Atari has a contract to modify its tank-attack video game for the training of real tank personnel. Combat conditions have been simulated in lifelike scenarios, with fighter pilots now playing video "games" for keeps. Journalist Francis X. Clines has commented that "a full-blown, realistic war seems possible for those who need one, replete with hostile missile hits and bomb targetings and blast flashes, with only bloodshed unprogrammed. The diplomats could then declare Videopeace."

CHAPTER 10

THE COMPUTER AND SOCIETY

As personal computers—the domesticated versions of the machines that run and oversee much of our lives—find their way into more homes and offices, computer technology is bound to becomes less intimidating; no longer will the computer be the distant, mysterious "thing." And in time, the computer will take its place among the airplane, automobile, and television as yet another ordinary wonder of the twentieth century.

But just as those other inventions have been mixed blessings, so this machine offers pitfalls as well as promise. In our rush to apply the computer to every aspect of our existence we may not have always thought out all the possible consequences of what we are doing.

Because we rely more on the computer than on any other machine, we are therefore more vulnerable to it as well. Computers are used to monitor and control much of our industrial civilization, and breakdowns can mean serious losses of time and money. In some cases these breakdowns can even be life threatening.

On the other hand, extensive use of computers can sometimes prove harmful—because they do work so well. For example, computerization can be a problem when private organizations use it solely to maximize profit, without consideration for the social consequences. The same machines can also cause problems when public institutions install them simply because they are available and can do the job. Whether its use is consciously planned because it serves someone's self-interest, or it is put on line simply because it's there and happens to speed things up, the computer can often pose a threat as well as offer a promise for a better future.

Unregulated or carelessly planned computer use often wreaks havoc in our lives. "You can be replaced by a machine" was the gallows humor of a generation ago, at the beginning of the computer era. That, of course, is no longer funny to the increasing number of unemployed who have lost their jobs to automation. At the very least this poor planning can inconvenience or outright hinder us when we can't straighten out a matter—with a utility company, for example—because their system is "down."

At its worst, computer misuse can threaten our civil liberties, insidiously affect the way we think, or even pose a danger to the earth's physical existence because of our overdependence on a computer-controlled nuclear missile warning system. The common thread that runs through all of this is not, of course, the willfulness of a machine, but rather our abdication of responsibility for the use of that machine—our stubborn adherence to the notion that computerization, wherever feasible, is inevitable, and that any negative consequences are simply a cross we must bear.

Artificial Intelligence

To many people, there has always been a mixture of threat and promise in the artificial intelligence field. Computers that imitate human reason can relieve us of many of the onerous, everyday burdens of running our society. But how many of us are entirely comfortable with the thought of being surrounded by machines that can "think"? Indeed, does it even make sense to use the word think when speaking of machines, since the ability to think is what distinguishes humans from nonhumans?

Proponents of machine intelligence point out that a program containing a conditional branch (an "if/ then" statement) enables the computer to make logical inferences. A prime example is the diagnostic programs by which computers systematically check a patient's symptoms against information stored in memory to determine the possible causes of an illness. Software enabling a computer to "learn" from experience has been around for some time; a pioneering effort was Arthur Samuel's checkers-playing program. Some advances have even been made in developing computer languages that can deal with the complexities of human languages—List Processing (or LISP) being one of the most notable examples.

Ultimately, those who defend the idea that computers can reason usually fall back on the test of machine intelligence devised by British mathematician Alan Turing. In this test, a computer and a human being are hidden from a second human who is to pose questions to each and then decide which respondent is wire and silicon and which flesh and blood. In other words, if a computer appears to be intelligent, then it is intelligent.

None of this is merely academic. At some point we may be called upon to decide whether or not we want to devote billions of tax dollars to probing the limits of machine intelligence. Will it be worth it? Which expert shall we listen to? Some say that build ing machines that can think is not only infantile but impractical as well. Science writer Fred Hapgood, in a 1974 article in the *Atlantic*, wrote (in reference to artificial intelligence) that, "Every culture has its juvenile embarrassments; misdirected enthusiasms which fail dramatically and in retrospect seem to say something humiliating about the civilization that pursued them." But there are those who disagree, MIT's Marvin Minsky—a brilliant scientist and one of the foremost authorities in the artificial intelligence field—among them. Minsky, who is fond of the outrageous and provocative remark, contends that thinking is not a monopoly of the human mind—which is, after all essentially nothing more than a "meat machine."

The field of artificial intelligence is not without its humor, however. A few years ago Joseph Weizenbaum, who was once an enthusiastic supporter of and contributor to research on machine intelligence and then split with his colleagues to become one of the field's severest critics, created a program called ELIZA, which simulated a psychotherapist. PARRY, a simulated paranoid personality developed by Ken Colby of Stanford University, was hooked up to ELIZA to produce a primitive, humorous demonstration of artificial intelligence. It produced the following:

P: In my opinion, you have a one-track mind.
E: What makes you think I have a one-track mind?
P: I used to go to the track every week.
E: What does that suggest to you?
P: I avoid race tracks now because the races are fixed.
E: Is that the real reason?
P: I'd rather not discuss it.

E: What else would you like to discuss?

P: That's something I don't want to go into.

This sort of thing is as intriguing as it is funny, and with a little imagination one might see here some possibilities for programs that could actually perform some useful work—although there are limits. Some writers, however, whose enthusiasm for thinking machines gets the better of their good judgment, do not know a joke when they see one. Thus a few years ago a prominent popularizer of science wrote that he could conceive of "the development of a network of computer psychotherapeutic terminals, something like arrays of large telephone booths, in which, for a few dollars a session, we would be able to talk with an attentive, tested, and largely nondirective psychotherapist."

For those raised on the image of the computer as a giant, omniscient brain, it can be especially satisfying to read about the machine that trips over its own wires. Alex Bernstein, who designed one of the first successful chess programs in the 1950s, recalls of those days that the machine's game-playing career started with a bug instead of a bang: "The very first move the machine ever made was to resign!" In truth, program refinements and hardware improvements since then have made computers imposing opponents for all but the very best players. Even the less-sophisticated chess software for personal computers will give you a hard time.

To think that computers might be able to learn, think, and imagine just as we do is to miss the point. Computers can "learn" in the sense that they can take limited types of experience into account when choosing to follow one path rather than another. That the computer can do in a second what none of us could ever do in a lifetime may predispose us to conclude that it can "think," but Peter H. Huyck and Nellie W. Kremenak in their book, *Design & Memory: Computer Programming in the 20th Century*, offer a useful corrective to that notion: "The machine can point to another address in memory, but it cannot point out into the world. The machine does not have access to the meaning of the symbols, in the same sense that a clock does not have access to time. People have access to meaning." And, in the end, the people who program the computer are the ones who do the thinking.

But what of the future? Given advances in technology—improvements in operating speed and information-handling capacity—will computers eventually be our mental equals? That is probably putting the question the wrong way. If what we mean by that is, "Can computers, under limited circumstances, imitate human reason?" then the answer is that they have already been doing so for quite some time. And they are likely to continue to do so as long as they are properly and imaginatively programmed by humans. Ample funds are being poured into this field by the U.S. Department of Defense, so we are likely to see more and increasingly complicated applications in the future.

The Computerized Bureaucracy

Large organizations, while using the computer to speed up data processing and handle volumes of records that might overwhelm a noncomputerized system, have also caused a decline in our quality of life by using this machine. Unfortunately, in many cases the computer has also served to enhance some of the negative qualities that, because of their very size, these organizations displayed in the first place.

The problem area here is the interaction between computers and bureaucracy. More than any other invention, the computer seems to have engendered in us a sense of passivity, a willingness to view the machine as an authority, and ourselves as powerless. The psychological aura that surrounds computers has been especially damaging when sewn into the fabric of bureaucracy, a social invention that substantially predates computers. We have, for example, met the computer-supported bureaucrat in our fight with the phone company over the long-distance call we never made but which has nevertheless appeared persistently on our bill; in our struggle with the government agency from which we can get no satisfaction because their computers have "fouled up"; and in our sometimes fruitless efforts to stop the magazine we subscribe to from appearing in our mailbox in triplicate, or to discover why it does not arrive at all.

It may seem that computers are a godsend to bureaucrats, who have a reputation for seeking the shortest distance between responsibility and its avoidance. But who's in charge here? Why do we accept weak explanations that so often attribute blame to an object that can't defend itself? Any time you call or write to a large organization with a question or a complaint, the odds are you will deal with a person, not a computer. The machines occasionally make errors—a fluctuation in the power supply can wipe out data in the computer's memory, for example—but the odds are greatly in favor of a human mistake when something goes wrong. Very likely it has been the "Garbage In/Garbage Out" principle in action; somebody may just have mistaken a "6" for a "9"—but that's all it takes to make several hundred thousand people miserable and frustrated when the computer faithfully compounds the error. But that doesn't let the person who answered your call or correspondence off the hook. These things *can* be traced and corrected. "It must have been the computer," or "the computer goofed" explain and excuse nothing. If this is as far as you get in such an encounter then insist on speaking to a manager or a supervisor. At no point will you be connected to a machine; eventually you will find a desk at which the buck will stop.

The Computer at Work

The use of computers on our jobs promises to bring substantial change in the way many of us make our living.

According to some, the workplace of the future may actually be quite a different one—the home. Many of us may be "telecommuting" from an "electronic cottage." Already a growing number of people work by sitting down at a computer terminal in their living rooms. Typists for the Continental Illinois Bank, for example, take dictation over the phone in their homes and use word processors to write and edit copy which is transmitted back to the bank's computers without a piece of paper ever being touched. But don't throw away your commuter ticket just yet. Because of the interactive nature of most jobs it is estimated that no more than fifteen percent of us will ever have this option.

Automation is an area in which the computer was once thought to offer almost nothing but promise. In the 1960s there was considerable speculation about the new and better world that would come from the application of computers to manufacturing: Aristotle's prediction that "When looms weave by themselves, man's slavery will end" actually seemed within reach. The temporary dislocation and trauma that might come with computerized automation seemed an acceptable trade-off for hard and dirty work no longer being the human lot. (Those who would be dislocated and traumatized had yet to be heard from.)

In the past few decades, as our economy has shifted from one based on the labor-intensive production of goods to one geared to capital-intensive manufacturing and the manipulation of information from which the most important product is service, work has indeed gotten "cleaner"; blue collars have disappeared or faded to white as fewer and fewer people get their hands dirty on the job. But we now seem to spend as much time pushing buttons as previous generations did moving heavy objects. The economic benefits of automation have been taken in the coin of greater productivity and profit, not more leisure.

Who made the decision in any given instance to replace workers with machines? Who opted for increased productivity rather than more leisure? These decisions have deeply affected our lives, and yet we so often think of them as something that has vaguely come about because of the computer, rather than the outcome of an individual or group pursuing a self-interested goal. General Motors, for example, hopes to make human workers and robots "interchangeable"; workers and computer-controlled machines would alternate on GM production lines. Not surprisingly, the United Auto Workers has taken a dim view of this and a UAW consultant has called the robots "power masquerading as technology."

Now that the Japanese are replacing fifteen-dollar-per-hour workers with robots that can be maintained for about one-third that cost, it is even more imperative that we deal with the social implications of computerization. Japanese workers have easily adapted to working next to robots. A Japanese psychologist has noted that some workers in his country actually "stroke" the metal automatons and greet them every day with a "Good morning."

We have reached a point in the economic integration of the world where such a basic change in production methods affects all of us. Competition with Japan and other industrialized nations will increase the pressure for maximum use of computer-controlled machinery. The use or nonuse of these machines should not be a phenomenon that just "happens."

Defenders of automation point out, correctly, that the computer often creates more jobs than it eliminates. But many people made obsolete along with those jobs may lack the educational background to take advantage of retraining; often retraining is not available to those who have lost their jobs to robots; frequently new jobs are located in distant places, which requires that families be uprooted and community ties broken. Automation is progress to those whose bread it butters, say its opponents; others may go hungry.

But none of this should be blamed on or even

remotely attributed to the computer. That would be confusing human thought, will, and action with inert machinery; philosophy and politics with technology. To automate or not is an economic choice and its effect is a political problem; the technology itself is simply a tool.

Computer Crime

Some of the new economic opportunities opened up by the computer certainly have nothing to do with productivity. Because computers make it possible to record and transfer huge amounts of money almost instantaneously, they also make it much easier than before to steal large sums. In an age of automated information processing, can automated theft be far behind?

The perfect crime is the one you can commit from your easy chair. Some corporate computer programs are so complicated and lengthy that a person skilled in the ways of the machine can create a "trapdoor"; when the program is run numbers are automatically added or subtracted and information created or erased, resulting in funds being shifted to a place where they don't belong. In this case "progress" means that the potential for easy theft of large sums has increased enormously.

Elaborate security codes are often required to gain access to corporate databases. Programs are written to watch over the running of other programs, leaving an audit trail to identify who has used the machine, when they used it, and how much time they spent on line. Companies especially sensitive about data security hire "computer buster" services to see if their systems can be penetrated and chinks in their digital armor thus exposed.

But even the most elaborate security systems can't anticipate all contingencies. In one case a clever pilferer got some information he wasn't supposed to have by instructing the computer itself to try every possible combination in its 5-digit access code until it hit the right one.

What you read and hear about electronic theft is just the tip of the iceberg. It is in the interest of a company—banks and brokerage firms, especially—not to publicize the fact that they have been victimized in this manner, lest their customers feel insecure about dealing with them. Often such losses are hushed up and police investigators encounter a stone wall when they try to get the company's cooperation. A corporation may even choose not to prosecute a thief if restitution is made and an explanation given of how the crime was committed.

Given the complexity and size of modern corporations, they will no doubt increase their use of computers to store and manipulate information. It's not unreasonable, therefore, to assume that those inclined to take advantage of the increased vulnerability of these organizations will enjoy increasing prosperity, since the speed, efficiency, and information-handling capacity of the computer make it tempting to extend its use.

There are no easy solutions to the dilemma this creates. At some point the benefits of the next opportunity to process data electronically must be weighed against the potential harm that can be caused. The efficiency of a machine reaches a point of diminishing return when it permits more profits to be drained off than it creates, not only undermining the health of a firm but also leading to increased prices for goods and services in order to make up for those losses.

<hr>

Civil Liberties

The computer's ability to store vast quantities of data in a relatively small amount of space and the ease with which that information can be accessed have made for greater efficiency in our large institutions. But this has also created potential legal and ethical problems: invasion of privacy and threats to our civil liberties.

Currently, over 4 billion records concerning individuals are stored in U.S. government computers. A late-1970s proposal to make those records accessible through one system called FEDNET was bottled up when Congress got wind of it. Since then the Reagan administration has proposed a National Recipient Information System that would keep tabs on every welfare recipient in the country, and the government has already begun to use IRS records to trace the whereabouts of young men who have not registered for the draft.

In 1956, the Law Enforcement Intelligence Unit, a private statewide organization of local government agencies in California, was set up to "promote the gathering, recording, investigating and exchange of confidential information not available through regular police channels concerning organized crime." The group's membership grew and spread out geographically over several states; it even managed to get some government grant money. By the 1970s it had computerized its files, which included the names of people whose politics the organization found distasteful, as well as those of known criminals. The Michigan State Legislature investigated it in 1979 and discovered files characterizing some of those under surveillance as patrons of "low-class colored bars," others as "pin-ball cheats," and one described as a "member of the Masonic Lodge, 32nd degree."

If you think the quirky mentality of this quasi-governmental group renders it less than threatening, consider this: Kenneth Laudon, a professor of sociology and statistics at the John Jay College of Criminal Justice in New York City, sampled the FBI's card file of criminal records and the similar but computerized files maintained by three states in conjunction with proposals that the FBI establish an Interstate Identification Index that would give on-line access to all state and federal criminal records. There was at least one error in fifty percent of the sample from one state, in eighty-two percent from the second, and in ninety percent from the third. The FBI's card file produced an error rate of seventy-four percent.

Computer-accessible personal data, by its very nature, can be a restraint on freedom. Former Senator Sam Ervin, chairman of the Senate Watergate Committee and a champion of civil liberties, put it eloquently in a 1973 speech:

> On the most general level it seems to me just plain unhealthy for some master computer to keep track of every detail of our lives—our words and deeds, our mistakes and failures, our weaknesses and our strengths. Some experts in the field of infor-

mation systems have suggested that massive data collection on every detail of each individual's life poses the danger of creating an "information prison" in which the individual is forever constrained by his past words and actions. What is lost in the process is the individual's capacity to grow and change, to define and redefine himself and to redeem past errors. There is something to be said for forgiving and forgetting and for the opportunity to start anew. That chance for a new start is, after all, the reason why many of our ancestors came to this country—to leave past lives and past mistakes behind, and to begin building a new life all over again.

The amount of data relating to our everyday activities, tastes, and opinions that is stored electronically will increase as we opt for such conveniences as electronic funds transfer and shopping at home through the use of the personal computer. Libraries are beginning to imprint a bar scan code in their books to facilitate check-out procedures and record keeping, making it easier to set up a database containing lists of what each patron has been reading. And it is not pleasant to think that the *New Yorker* cartoon which depicts a couple choosing a movie and in which the wife is saying "What would look good on our dossier?" could in fact foreshadow our future.

Computers and Our Values

Perhaps the most far-reaching—and the most subtle—effect that computers have had and will continue to have on us involves our way of seeing the world. Technology has always influenced our values: the machinery of the nineteenth century Industrial Revolution, for example, made efficiency the yardstick against which we measure so many things.

How has the computer changed our basic way of living? Have those changes all been desirable? If they have not, is there anything we can do about it without foregoing the advantages of the machine?

Whether or not computers will ever come close to being able to think as we do, it is clear that they have already affected our thoughts—and our language, as witnessed by the use of "input," "output," and "interface" to describe human actions. It is not unusual for computer metaphors to be used to describe mental activities that one would think are quite remote from machinery. The catalog of a mail-order bookseller, for example, recently described the thesis of a book called *Dreaming and Memory: A New Information-Processing Model* in this way: "Dreams serve an information-processing function by matching present and past experience in determining what information will be filtered through for storage in permanent memory." Is this really a healthy way for human beings to think about themselves?

Computers are going to play an increasingly greater role in education; of that there can be little doubt. But they are also, for some, beginning to play a part in defining the very nature of the educational process. Herbert Simon, a Nobel Prize winner in economics and a prominent figure in artificial intelligence research, says the computer has changed the meaning of "knowing" from "having information stored in one's memory" to "the process of having access to information." An educator who extended this metaphor from knowing to learning—education as "basically an information-transfer process"—earned the disdain of *New York Times* columnist Russell Baker, who wrote: "Education is not like a decal, to be slipped off a piece of stiff paper and pasted on the back of the skull. The point of education is to waken innocent minds to a suspicion of information."

In our society, the informal passing along of information and values—education outside the classroom—has also been influenced by the computer. This may or may not be a positive thing, but the fact is that it often happens by default, unexamined or not considered to be something over which we have any control.

The arcade video games, for example, that have been much criticized for their hypnotic hold on adolescents who spend long hours and a good deal of money playing them, are more than just a form of recreation that is of questionable value to some: they do also have a teaching function. We know that athletic games teach cooperativeness and fair play. But what do video games teach? Do they have a message? Substantial criticism has been made of their violent and warlike themes. Even the sentimentalized Pac-Man, whose cheery yellow silhouette has appeared on T-shirts and other objects, has a bellicose moral: eat or be eaten, the law of the jungle.

But it may also be that video games teach another way of looking at the world. The best games, although they are clever and inventive and require a good deal of manual dexterity and quick reflexes (they may even prove useful in training the physically handicapped), are impossible to win. The real object of the game is simply to delay the inevitable annihilation, not to emerge victorious. The view of life inherent in these contests also contains an element of paranoia: in the video game world you have enemies who come at you ceaselessly from all sides; you may destroy many of them, but in the end they always get you.

The ultimate effect of early and continuous exposure to computers on the minds and personalities of children is not yet clear. Some MIT research suggests that there could be an important psychological impact. What, for example, does it mean to "be alive"? Computers can easily be made to speak, and to some children that may be confusing because speech seems to be an attribute of living things only. The national news magazines have sensed some adult anxiety on this subject, and *Time* recently sought to quell such fears by quoting a high school student who reassured his elders that the younger generation, as a result of exposure to computers, would not "be weird, or have green faces, or somehow be abnormal."

Is the world orderly, predictable, and precise? Or do our lives and surroundings really reflect chance and surprise? These are the kinds of questions that are at the heart of philosophy. Even before the advent of the computer, there was a mathematical, linear, and non-interpretive thinking style which science historian Derek de Solla Price has pointed out can be traced back to Babylonian culture. Another way of looking at the world—more holistic, nonlinear, with an emphasis on imagery—predominated in ancient Greece. Neither mode has ever claimed sole domain over any culture, but the computer's established role in our culture is already making the mathematical and linear approach considerably more pervasive for us. What if this really got out of hand?

This phenomenon may already be showing up in our romance with model building—the simulation of real-life events by mathematical equations that has been the backbone of much recent research in the social sciences. Newspapers often refer to models of the economy that tell us how things are going to be in the coming year. When used intelligently they give us more control over our lives; they make the unknown more predictable. But at the same time they would make us more vulnerable if we were to mindlessly increase our dependence on them.

One problem with relying on such formalistic ways of viewing the world is that they are dangerously subject to the effect of the "Garbage In/Garbage Out" principle. Models are based on past facts and are supposed to aid us in predicting what is to come. But as the authors of *Energy Future*, a book about a field in which prediction has run wild, point out, that is like "looking forward through a rear-view mirror." Many of these models look impressive with their computer-generated numbers, but they may have no more predictive power than a fortune cookie.

More fundamentally, models impose a digital order on an analog world. As with any abstraction or theory, they can be useful *if* we retain a sense of their limits. If we used computer models to describe the world we are saying that what we are dealing with is quantifiable, logical, and systematic—that things are either true or false, up or down, one or the other (1 or 0). This is fine as far as it goes, as long as we don't get too swept away by the prospect of neatness and certainty and forget how much of reality is mystery, chance idiosyncracy, ambivalence, and the irrational.

Our Lives in Their Hands

Increasingly, computers are being used to monitor and operate virtually every material component of our civilization. They are singularly reliable machines, yet they can and do break. Although the odds are greatly against that happening to any one computer at a given time (and backup systems for machines used in sensitive applications make that even more unlikely), remember what happened at the Three Mile Island nuclear power plant.

Relatively subtle shifts in the voltage feeding computers can bring these machines down. Static electricity can alter data, and air-conditioning failures can cause computers to overheat. The interaction of long and complex programs with hardware can even produce strange and unanticipated results when the computer must deal with a situation or conditions unplanned for by its designers; such interactions are known as "sneak circuits."

As we all know, the effect of a computer system's failure has the potential to be disastrous. On June 3, 1980, and again three days later, the telecommunications system that connects the computers in Cheyenne Mountain, Colorado, headquarters of the North American Air Defense Command, with the Strategic Air Command in Omaha and the government communications center near Washington, D.C., mistakenly flashed a warning that Soviet missiles had been launched toward the United States. In the three minutes that it took to ascertain that the alert was false, one hundred B-52 bombers armed with nuclear weapons were prepared for take-off, the president's airborne command post—the "doomsday" plane—was readied for action, and in missile launching sites across the country personnel were notified of the possibility that they might have to turn the keys that would launch their weapons. What really happened? A malfunctioning forty-six cent integrated circuit component had momentarily edged us toward the brink of nuclear conflict. As the time it takes to reach an enemy with nuclear weapons grows continually shorter, the temptation to adopt a "launch on warning" strategy can only increase. And notwithstanding the government's reassurance to the American people that we were nowhere near World War III, then Secretary of Defense Harold Brown admitted to the *Wall Street Journal* a month later that greater care would have to be taken not to "let computers make the decision as to when we go to war."

A Tool Like Any Other

The computer—the machine that makes the prodigious and amazing merely routine—has, like much of our technology, been a mixed blessing. It has done, and will continue to do, much for us. But misused, it can be the source of untold mischief and even destruction. A century before the invention of the modern computer Henry David Thoreau warned that thoughtless use of technology might make us the "tool of our tools." We are now no less helpless in the face of this machine than Thoreau's generation was when dealing with the technology of the early industrial era.

The way to use anything properly is to understand what it is and what it can do. But in the face of fear and ignorance, anything can be made to seem omnipotent and threatening. Some years ago Stanley Kubrick made a very successful film called *2001: A Space Odyssey.* Based on a story by Arthur C. Clarke, it featured a vigilant, obtrusive, neurotic, and finally, murderous computer named HAL. To drive home the point that computers can pose real problems for society, there was embedded in the name of the machine a reference to the real-life corporation that for many symbolizes the world of computers, a company whose image was one of distance, cold efficiency, impersonality, and conformity: its initials are the letters that follow next alphabetically after H, A, and L.

There is nothing inevitable about HAL's world; neither are the negative aspects of the present use of computers, dominated and symbolically embodied by HAL's alphabetical shadow, so entrenched in our lives that we can't alter them. Political and economic decisions are, after all, made by people and not machines. There's no real reason why we can't enjoy all the promise offered by computers while avoiding the potential threats their use may pose.

GLOSSARY

A

Alphanumeric The set of characters not only containing numbers and letters, but also spaces, and other punctuation marks.

Analog Computer A computer which uses continuous variable physical quantities to describe data.

Artificial Intelligence A discipline concerning the implementation of intelligent, humanlike problem-solving capabilities in machines. Such tasks include games, natural language capabilities and question answering.

Assembly Language (or *Assembler Language*) A mnemonic representation of a computer's machine language, which is easier to code than the 1s and 0s of machine language but not as accessible as high-level languages such as FORTRAN.

B

BASIC Beginner's All-purpose Symbolic Instruction Code. A fairly easy-to-learn, high-level computer language that is frequently used in personal computers.

Batch Processing A data processing operation whereby data is accumulated and then brought to a computer to be processed. The user has no access to the machine during processing, and output is not always readily available. Batch processing is useful for dealing with large amounts of data when speed is not essential.

Baud A unit of measurement for data transmission, representing bits per second.

Binary Number System A number system based on two, using only the numbers 1 and 0.

Bit Short for *bi*nary dig*it*, the smallest amount of information a computer can handle. Symbolically represented in two states, either 0 or 1.

Bubble Memory A computer memory which uses magnetic "bubbles"—locally magnetized areas that can move about in a magnetic material. Because it is possible to control the reading in and out of these bubbles within the magnetic material, very high-capacity memories can be built.

Buffer A device that temporarily stores data. The buffer is often used to hold data being transmitted from a computer to a printer, since the computer sends it out much faster than the printer can print it.

Bug An error in a program or a machine malfunction that produces undesirable or incorrect results.

Byte A group of binary digits, or bits —usually eight—treated as a whole by the machine. Usually, one alphanumeric character (a letter, number or symbol) can be stored in one byte.

C

Central Processing Unit (CPU) The heart of the computer. It controls the function of all other parts of the machine and performs arithmetic and logical operations on data.

COBOL COmmon Business-Oriented Language. A high-level English-like programming language widely used for business applications.

Compiler A computer program that translates a high-level language into machine language.

Computer A machine that processes numbers and words according to a set of instructions (program) stored in the machine. Computers are usually classified, in order of descending size and power, as mainframe, minicomputer and microcomputer (personal computer).

Conditional Branch A step in a computer program at which point the machine will do one of two things, depending upon whether or not a specified condition has been satisfied. This is the means by which logic is built into a program.

CRT *(Cathode Ray Tube) Screen* Similar to a television screen; displays input and output. Sometimes called a VDT, or visual display terminal.

D

Daisy Wheel See **Printer.**

Data Processing The conversion of raw data into useful information.

Database A systematically organized computerized collection of information stored in a way that parallels common office files. "File" is a general category; "record" is a unit of the file; "field" contains information about the record.

Debugging The process of eliminating errors from a computer program.

Dedicated Devoted to only one function. A dedicated word processor, for example, can do word processing only and is not a general-purpose computer.

Digital Computer A computer that operates with numbers expressed directly as digits.

Disk A disk coated with a magnetic substance, which is used to store information that must be accessed quickly. Information is recorded magnetically on either plastic ("floppy") or metal disks. Plastic disks are available in 3½", 5¼", and 8" sizes, and hold less than one megabyte each; hard metal disks store up to several hundred megabytes apiece. The hard disks used with personal computers are called Winchesters.

Distributed Processing A system by which data can be processed at various points throughout an organization instead of on just one central computer.

Dot Matrix See **Printer.**

E

EDP Electronic data processing.

F

Flowchart A diagrammatic method of representing the logic flow of a computer program or system. Programmers use flowcharts to guide them in coding a program into a computer language.

FORTRAN FORmula TRANslator. The first widely used high-level computer language. FORTRAN was developed by IBM in the middle 1950s and is still used extensively for mathematical and scientific applications.

H

Hardware The physical equipment of a computer system, exclusive of the software, or programs, that make it run.

High-Level Language A programming language such as FORTRAN, which is modeled after a human language.

I

Input Information (data or programs) entered into a computer for processing or storage.

Integrated Circuits A complete solid state, complex circuit able to perform all the functions of conventional circuits including transistors, diodes, etc. An integrated circuit is contained in one extremely small package.

J

Joystick A device such as a lever, often similar to an automobile gearshift, used in video games to direct the computer to move a graphically depicted object on the screen in a particular direction.

K

Keypunch A machine used to code computer-readable information on a special card in a pattern of punched holes.

Kilobyte Literally, one thousand bytes; actually, 1024. A computer's random access memory (RAM) is usually described as having so many Kilobytes, or "Ks," as in 64K.

L

Light Pen A device used to enter information into a computer by pointing at a spot on a terminal screen. It is often used in creating graphics.

M

Machine Language The pattern of 1s and 0s (bits) directly recognizable by a computer as instructions.

Magnetic Tape Magnetic medium which can be read sequentially. Although tape can store more information per unit of space than disks—and is thus useful for archival storage—it is not convenient for accessing specific data quickly.

Mainframe See **Computer.**

Megabyte One million bytes.

Microcomputer The smallest classification of computer. Home computers fall into this category. See also **Computer.**

Microprocessor An integrated circuit containing the basic logic, storage and arithmetic functions of a computer.

Microsecond One millionth of a second.

Millisecond One thousandth of a second.

Minicomputer See **Computer.**

Modem From MOdulator-DEModulator. A device used to transmit computer data over telephone lines.

N

Nanosecond One billionth of a second.

Network An interconnected system of computers and associated equipment, often in different locations.

O

On line Data processing by which the user communicates with the computer directly: input is entered at a terminal and output appears shortly thereafter.

Operating System The controlling software of a machine that organizes and controls the execution of all other programs run on that system.

Optical Character Recognition *(OCR)* A process by which characters printed in a special type font are scanned by a reading device and entered directly into the computer. OCR characters can also be read by humans.

Output The results of the computer's processing of data, displayed in a form recognizable to humans—by CRT or printer, for example.

P

Pascal A high-level programming language named after French mathematician Blaise Pascal (1623–1662).

Peripheral Devices Those parts of a computer system—printers, modems and disk drives, for example—that are connected to but not part of the central processing unit.

Personal Computer A microcomputer designed for use in a small business or the home, or for handling limited tasks in a large organization.

Printer A device used to produce paper copies (printouts) of computer output. Dot matrix models, in which pins strike a ribbon to produce characters, and daisy wheels, which hold characters on petal-like spokes, are the most common types.

Programmer The person who codes a program into a language that can be used by the computer.

R

RAM See **Random Access Memory.**

Random Access Memory *(RAM)* The internal computer memory that stores data and programs currently in use, and which can be both read from and written to. Usually RAM is volatile, that is, its contents are erased when the computer is turned off.

Read Only Memory *(ROM)* Internal computer memory whose contents cannot usually be altered, and which can only be read from. ROM stores programs the computer uses for its everyday operations.

ROM See **Read Only Memory.**

S

Semiconductor A substance used in transistors whose medium resistance to electricity makes it useful for regulating current flow.

Software The programs that instruct the computer, step-by-step, to perform a series of operations.

Solid State Electronic components which, unlike vacuum tubes, are made of solid materials.

Systems Analyst The person who analyzes a specific need of an organization with an aim toward computerizing its operation.

T

Telecommunication Communicating over a distance, whereby computer data may be sent via telephone lines or by microwave.

Teletext A noninteractive computer system by which information may be selected for viewing on a television screen.

Terminal A device capable of sending and receiving information from a computer. It is normally equipped with a keyboard input, and a CRT or printer output.

Time Sharing An on-line system in which many users at remote terminals share the facilities of one central computer.

Transistor A semiconductor device which replaced the vacuum tube as the basis for computer technology. Machines using transistors are known as "second generation."

U

Universal Product Code The pattern of black bars stamped on consumer goods that can be scanned by a reading device to enter product identification, price, and other information into a computer.

User-friendly Hardware or software that can be easily used by a computer novice.

V

Vacuum Tube First type of electronic element used in computers for memory, etc.

Videotex An interactive system of home television, computers, and telecommunications lines which enables individuals to gain access to and alter computer data. Applications include shopping and banking at home.

W

Winchester Disk See **Disk.**

Word A collection of bits which are treated as a whole by a computer.

Word Processing The manipulation, storage, and retrieval of text for letters, reports, etc. by computer control. Many automatic features such as margin adjustments, deletions and insertions are possible with such a system.

INDEX